STUDIES IN THE HISTORY

The Lincolnshire Wolds in the Nineteenth Century

CHARLES K. RAWDING

STUDIES IN THE HISTORY OF LINCOLNSHIRE 1

THE LINCOLNSHIRE WOLDS
IN THE
NINETEENTH CENTURY

CHARLES K. RAWDING

Lincoln
HISTORY OF LINCOLNSHIRE COMMITTEE
2001

Published 2001 by
The History of Lincolnshire Committee, Jews' Court, Steep Hill, Lincoln

© 2001 by The History of Lincolnshire Committee and Charles K. Rawding

ISBN   hard back   0 902668 20 X
ISBN   paperback   0 902668 21 8

Cover illustrations:
Lincolnshire cornfield near Horncastle, c. 1815, Peter De Wint; detail. By kind permission of the Lincolnshire County Council (Educational and Cultural Services Directorate), Usher Gallery, Lincoln
Saunder's map of Lincolnshire, 1836, detail. Private collection; by courtesy of Steven Smallwood

Title page vignette:
Steam threshing at what is thought to be Swallow Grange, 19th century wood engraving. By kind permission of Lincolnshire County Council (Educational and Cultural Services Directorate), Museum of Lincolnshire Life, Lincoln

Cover design by Max Marschner Graphics, Lincoln LN5 8PN
Typeset and produced for the publisher by Yard Publishing Services, Sudbury CO10 2AG
Printed by Interprint, Malta

British Cataloguing-in-Publication Data
    A catalogue record for this book is obtainable from the British Library

TO KEN PARROTT

An avid reader of history,
Lincolnshire through and through,
and a great neighbour.

CONTENTS

FIGURES

TABLES

ABBREVIATIONS

AHR	*Agricultural History Review*
BPP	British Parliamentary Papers
CEB	Census enumerators books
CP	The papers of the Clarke family, formerly of Binbrook Manor
GFP	*Grimsby Free Press*
JRASE	*Journal of the Royal Agricultural Society of England*
LAO	Lincolnshire Archives Office
LC	*Lincolnshire Chronicle*
LH	*Lincolnshire Historian*
LHA	*Lincolnshire History and Archaeology*
LNLA	*Louth and North Lincolnshire Advertiser*
LRSM	*Lincoln, Rutland and Stamford Mercury*
MRWM	*Market Rasen Weekly Mail*
PRO	Public Record Office

FOREWORD

`Studies in the History of Lincolnshire' is a series of substantial scholarly books, which illuminate the history of Lincolnshire at different periods in the past.

Charles Rawding's study of the Lincolnshire Wolds in the 19th century is the first volume to be published in the series. It shows how the Wolds developed in the 19th century, and in particular it reveals how today's historic landscape evolved during a period of rapid and profound rural change. The book examines the landscape, life on the Wolds, the roles of landowners, tenant farmers and labourers, the market towns and their people, and the cultural and social life of the region. The study of individual regions such as the Wolds enables us to understand more about the long-term evolution of English society, and Dr Rawding shows just how distinctive life was in this particular part of Lincolnshire.

John V. Beckett
Nottingham, July 2001

ACKNOWLEDGEMENTS

This book developed out of my doctoral thesis, which was undertaken at the University of Sussex during the 1980s. It would not have been possible without the guidance and support of my supervisor, Professor Brian Short. I would like to thank Dr Dennis Mills and Mr Rex Russell for their help and encouragement throughout the project. I am grateful to Professor John Beckett for his editorial assistance in the later stages of the book; his advice and encouragement has undoubtedly improved the finished product.

As is inevitable when undertaking research of this type, I have received a great deal of help from a large number of people. The WEA classes of Keelby and Binbrook and the support of Mr Geoff Bryant were important during the early stages of the work. The late Mr Michael Sleight provided me with unlimited access to his large library and it is a very real regret that he did not live to see the finished product. Mrs Nicola Clarke, formerly of Binbrook Manor, Mr James Milligan-Manby of Thorganby Hall, and Mr Alec Thomson of Keelby all provided me with access to family papers. I would also like to thank my cartographer Ann Chapman for her work in producing all the maps and text figures.

Finally, I would like to thank my wife Helen for her support and forbearance over the last few years as the book has slowly materialized.

Figure 11 is published by kind permission of the owners, Hetts Johnson Whiting of Brigg. All other acknowledgements to sources are made in the captions to the figures. I thank all the institutions and individuals who have allowed me to use their material.

Charles K. Rawding
July 2001

INTRODUCTION

To the uninitiated, the cliché that Lincolnshire is a flat county akin to the Low Countries can be countered best in two ways. A brisk walk to the top of Steep Hill affirms the magnificent location of the cathedral high above the River Witham. Equally, a drive across the Wolds tests the ability of the average Midlands-based car to pull its caravan up Willingham Hill on its way to the coast, while the descent through South Elkington to Louth is hard work for the best of brakes.

The Wolds stand out, quite literally, from the rest of east Lincolnshire. A drive along the three principal north–south routes that run the length of the Wolds gives a sample of both the diversity of the scenery and the unity that clearly separates the region from its neighbours. The High Street from Caistor towards Horncastle provides clear views of the scarp slope of the hills with lower-lying land to the west while the rolling hills spread eastwards. From the Bluestone Heath road running along the spine of the Wolds, the scenery changes from the higher less-dissected hills of the north to the lower, gentler, rolling scenery in the valleys of rivers such as the Bain. To the east, the Barton Street provides a view of the dip slope of the Wolds as they rise out of the outer marshes through little-known parishes such as Hawerby and North Ormsby.

The Lincolnshire Wolds is a distinctive 'pays', a physical region (see Figure 1) distinguished clearly from the neighbouring marshes to the east and the sandy moors to the west. The region forms the highest ground in eastern England between Yorkshire and Kent. It is essentially an upland area of just over 350 square miles, some 45 miles in length and between five and eight miles wide. The landscape has been shaped by its varied underlying geology and the complex glacial and periglacial processes which transformed the topography during the last glaciation. The area basically comprises a chalk plateau with a steep scarp slope to the west. From this western edge, a dip slope ranging between 50m and

Figure 1 The Lincolnshire Wolds: Physical Regions

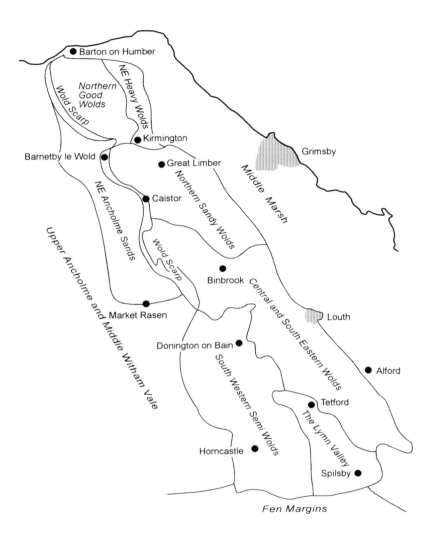

Fig. 1   The Lincolnshire Wolds: physical regions

120m extends eastwards. The northern wolds reach a peak of about 100m above Saxby All Saints, falling to as low as 20m in the Barnetby Gap before climbing to heights of more than 90m at Bigby Top. The Wolds are at their highest between Caistor and South Willingham, the highest point being 168m at Normanby Top.[1]

Much of the area can be described as a smooth, rolling, chalk plateau, although characteristic of the scarp slope are landslips and slumping giving a more hummocky appearance, particularly between Caistor and North Willingham. The scarp slope is much less pronounced south of Sixhills. The south-western Wolds are lower and glacial till overlays the chalk. Here, the drainage basin of the River Bain breaks up the plateau and provides a more undulating landscape with villages in the valley bottoms. At its southern margins, the Wolds descend into the Fens and the Middle Marsh, with a distinct dividing line only broken by the River Lymn and its tributaries flowing southwards to form the Steeping River.[2]

Within the Wolds there is considerable landscape variety (see Figure 3). The area is a smooth chalk tableland with very few villages. The action of streams cutting down through the chalk has had a significant influence on settlement patterns, with villages being located in the valleys or along the spring-line, as obtaining water has always been a problem. Nevertheless, some villages are also found in the dry valleys, as with the appropriately named Driby. Lines of small settlements are discernible east of Caistor in valleys leading to the marshes and converging on Swallow or Hatcliffe. Along the Wold Scarp, there is a chain of villages that follows the spring-line from South Ferriby through Barnetby Le Wold to Nettleton. Further south the line continues, but less clearly, through Walesby to Sixhills. The south-western Wolds is characterized by dispersed villages and small settlements. In the central areas, villages are more frequently found in the valleys. To the south, villages are particularly numerous along the southern edge and in the valleys of the Lymn and its tributaries. Generally speaking, greater population densities were found in the southern Wolds where the landscape is more varied as a result of the work of rivers carving valleys and providing more readily available sources of water.[3]

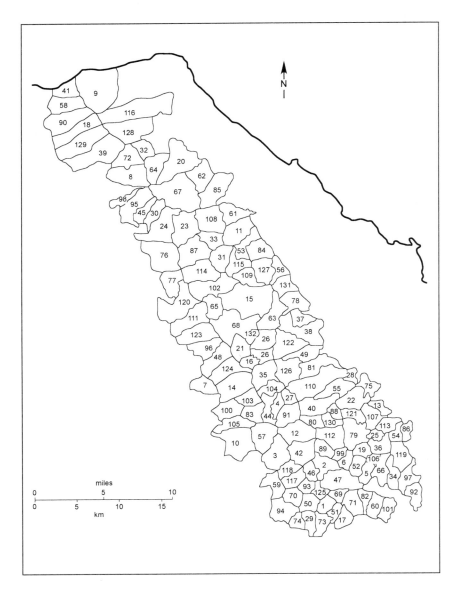

Fig. 2 The Lincolnshire Wolds: parishes
For key see opposite

1.	Asgarby	45.	Grasby	89.	Salmonby
2.	Ashby Puerorum	46.	Greetham	90.	Saxby
3.	West Ashby	47.	Hagwothingham	91.	Scamblesby
4.	Asterby	48.	Hainton	92.	Scremby
5.	Aswardby	49.	Hallington	93.	Scrafield
6.	Bag Enderby	50.	Hameringham	94.	Scrivelsby
7.	East Barkwith	51.	Hareby	95.	Searby cum Owmby
8.	Barnetby	52.	Harrington	96.	Sixhills
9.	Barton	53.	Hatcliffe	97.	Skendelby
10.	Baumber	54.	Haugh	98.	Somerby
11.	Beelsby	55.	Haugham	99.	Somersby
12.	Belchford	56.	Hawerby cum Beesby	100.	Sotby
13.	Belleau	57.	Hemingby	101.	Spilsby
14.	Benniworth	58.	Horkstow	102.	Stainton le Vale
15.	Binbrook	59.	Horncastle	103.	Market Stainton
16.	Biscathorpe	60.	Hundleby	104.	Stenigot
17.	(Old) Bolingbroke	61.	Irby	105.	Gt Sturton
18.	Bonby	62.	Keelby	106.	Sutterby
19.	Brinkhill	63.	Kelstern	107.	Swaby
20.	Brocklesby	64.	Kirmington	108.	Swallow
21.	Burgh on Bain	65.	Kirmond Le Mire	109.	Swinhope
22.	Burwell	66.	Langton by Partney	110.	Tathwell
23.	Cabourne	67.	Great Limber	111.	Tealby
24.	Caistor	68.	Ludford	112.	Tetford
25.	Calceby	69.	Lusby	113.	South Thoresby
26.	Calcethorpe	70.	Mareham on the Hill	114.	Thoresway
27.	Cawkwell	71.	Mavis Enderby	115.	Thorganby
28.	Little Cawthorpe	72.	Melton Ross	116.	Thornton Curtis
29.	Caxby Pluckacre	73.	Miningsby	117.	High Toynton
30.	Clixby	74.	Moorsby	118.	Low Toynton
31.	Croxby	75.	Muckton	119.	Ulceby nr Spilsby
32.	Croxton	76.	Nettleton	120.	Walesby
33.	Cuxwold	77.	Normanby le Wold	121.	Walmsgate
34.	Dalby	78.	North Ormsby	122.	Welton le Wold
35.	Donington on Bain	79.	South Ormsby	123.	North Willingham
36.	Driby	80.	Oxcombe	124.	South Willingham
37.	North Elkington	81.	Raithby cum Maltby	125.	Winceby
38.	South Elkington	82.	Raithby	126.	Withcall
39.	Elsham	83.	Ranby	127.	Wold Newton
40.	Farforth cum Maidenwell	84.	East Ravendale	128.	Wootton
41.	South Ferriby	85.	Riby	129.	Worlaby nr Brigg
42.	Fulletby	86.	Rigsby	130.	Worlaby nr Thetford
43.	Gayton le Wold	87.	Rothwell	131.	Wyham cum Cadeby
44.	Goulceby	88.	Ruckland	132.	East Wykeham

Fig. 2 continued   Key to the Lincolnshire Wolds parishes

To the immediate west of the upland lies a belt of wind-blown sand known as the Ancholme Sands which merges to the south of Market Rasen with the Middle Witham Vale. Here the land is much lower lying. To the east, the lower-lying chalk of the dip slope is overlain by glacial till and reclaimed salt marsh which forms the Middle Marsh.

In the 18th century, the Wolds was dominated by large, poorly worked farms but was then transformed by the mid 19th century into an area of rapid and disproportionately significant farming improvement, with large farms worked progressively. These changes led to a skewed social structure, hardly any towns or industry, and an almost total dominance of good quality agricultural practice. Only indirectly touched by the industrial revolution and processes of urbanization, yet the area contributed massively to economic change in the period by pushing up the output of the land. Only at the end of the 19th century did this progress falter as the area fell foul of agricultural depression.

The distinctive atmosphere of the Wolds has been captured in the paintings of Peter de Wint (1784–1849) whose *Lincolnshire Landscape* and *Harvest Field* show, respectively, the harvest on top of the Wolds and the Wolds escarpment from below.[4] Even better known as representations of the specific characteristics of the region are the poems of Tennyson.

> On either side of the river lie
> Long fields of barley and of rye,
> That clothe the wold and meet the sky,
> And through the field the road runs by.
>
> *The Lady of Shalott* [5]

> By thirty hills I hurry down,
> Or slip between the ridges
> By twenty thorpes, a little town
> And half a hundred bridges,
> Till last by Phillips farm I flow
> To join the brimming river,
> For men may come and men may go,
> But I go on for ever.
>
> *The Brook* [6]

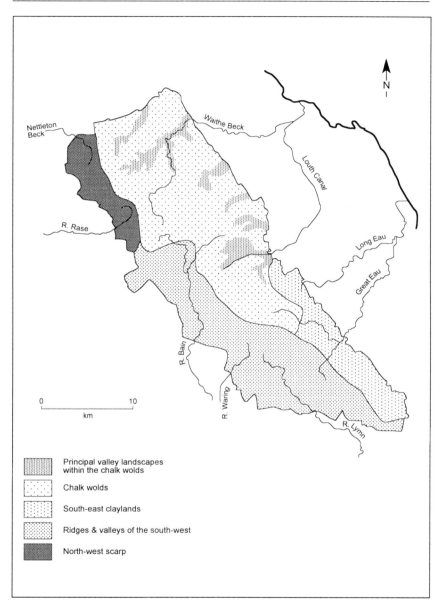

Fig. 3   Landscape character areas
Source: adapted from The Countryside Commission,
The Lincolnshire Wolds landscape, p. 14

Local distinctiveness is essentially about place, about the commonplace as well as the rare, the everyday as much as the endangered, and the ordinary as much as the spectacular. The landscape of the 19th century was a cultural landscape held together by the traces of parliamentary enclosure, the straight roads, wide verges and whitethorn hedges, the requirements of the farmer and the houses of his labourer. It contained the manors of the wealthy, emparked and screened by discreet planting of trees which further supplied the habitats for fox and game. It housed the agricultural workforce and the rural poor in its villages and hamlets. The larger villages and small towns acted as markets for produce and centres for services and were inextricably intertwined within this landscape.[7]

It was a landscape bound by dialect too, as wonderfully illustrated in the writings of Tennyson. It was the consequence of layer upon layer of history evolving and interlinked. Change, symbolism, and significance cling to seemingly ordinary buildings, trees, artefacts. The Wolds of Lincolnshire are similar to, yet different from the neighbouring Wolds of Yorkshire to the north, and the Chilterns and Berkshire Downs to the south. Their greater geological complexity provides a distinctiveness to the landscape on to which layers of human activity have been applied over the centuries.

Although the geology of the area has had a significant influence on the way in which the land has been developed over time, human influence on the development of the distinctive sense of place created should not be overlooked. Landlords were able to exert a power not only over the social agenda, but also a control over the physical landscape, creating a powerful visual imagery that reflected and glorified their status. They created parks and monuments, mansions, and workers' cottages and left an indelible print on the landscape of the area they controlled. It was their policies and their joint investments with their tenants which led to the development of an agrarian landscape characterized by large farms and profitable mixed farming. It was this landscape, the landscape of the lord, which was juxtaposed against a different landscape which evolved where the landownership structure was more fragmented and the major landowners and tenant farmers were far less dominant. The crowded, tumble-down cottages of

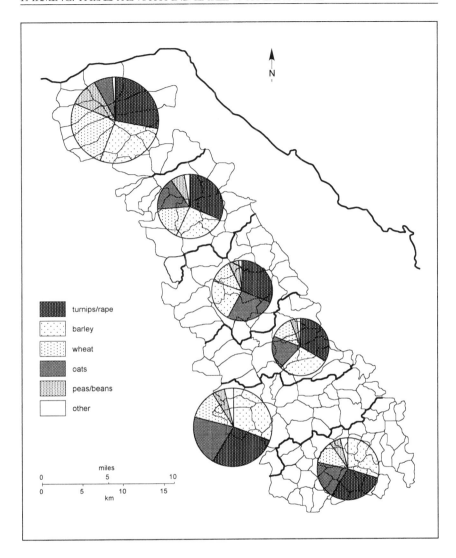

Fig. 4   Agricultural land in the Lincolnshire Wolds, 1801
Source: PRO. HO 67 Home Office Acreage Returns 1801

majority of the rotations described by Young for the area include one, if
not two, turnip crops in a four or five course rotation. The introduction
of turnips enabled sheep to be folded on the Wolds rather than being

taken to the marshes to be fattened. The second largest acreage was barley which, although less profitable than wheat, could at this time be grown more successfully on the thin chalky soils of the Wolds. Wheat yields were more variable; as a result, at the start of the century, it was still considered to be a high-risk crop by Wolds farmers.[7]

Some cattle were kept. Indeed, Thomas Bates of Worlaby had an offer of 1,000 guineas for a Lincolnshire shorthorn at Charles Colling's sale in 1810. However, rabbits were of greater significance at the beginning of the century. Young states: 'From Louth to Caistor, eighteen miles, ten of it are warrens.' At Binbrook in 1804, most of a 1,640 acre estate was a well-stocked rabbit warren. At Withcall, 2,600 couples were kept on 1,000 acres, a density of five rabbits to the acre. During the early years of the century, rabbit warrens were often incorporated into the mixed farming system of the area. For instance, Holdgate, the tenant of a 3,000 acre warren farm at Thoresway, had 1,700 acres under silver rabbits, 850 acres of corn, 950 acres of grass, turnips, and seed and 700 sheep. He was also one of the first farmers in the area to experiment with a water-powered threshing mill. The majority of the warrens were well managed and profitable. However, changing fashion led to a decline in demand for silver grey rabbit fur, while rabbit meat as a cheap meat for the urban classes was replaced by mutton. As a result, the value of the warrens fell. The falling price of rabbits combined with high grain prices during the Napoleonic Wars (see Figure 5) meant that many farmers were finding it more profitable to convert their land to grain or turnips, as at Stainton Le Vale, where land formerly warren was now under turnips. Young notes that the Rev. Mr Alington at Swinhope considered this 'the most expeditious way of bringing any land that has long been under rabbit ... into cultivation'.[8]

The high prices obtained for grain, combined with significant improvements in cultivation techniques, led to large areas of marginal land being taken into cultivation. For instance, between 1790 and 1804, on the Manners estate in the parishes of Revesby, Salmonby, Rigsby, and Alford, land formerly used as sheep walks was ploughed and new barns and extra farmsteads built.

Parliamentary enclosure over the period 1760–1830 assisted the transformation. Nationally, 3,721 Acts of parliamentary enclosure were

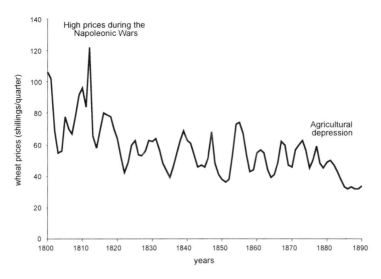

Fig. 5   Changes in wheat prices at Louth Market, 1800–1890

passed during the period. In Lincolnshire as a whole 313 Acts were passed during this period covering about one-third of the land in the county. 'Open unhedged fields and commons were planted with literally hundreds of kilometres of hawthorn hedges. New Georgian manors, parks and farmsteads were established often away from the villages … Straight drove roads up to 20m in width were built, between newly planted hedges.' This transformation was particularly marked in the central and northern areas of the Wolds. The south-western Wolds had a more wooded, enclosed, pastoral, and settled landscape where the changes were less dramatic.[9]

Measures such as these created a new agrarian landscape across the Wolds. Pusey, writing in 1843, estimated that 230,000 acres on the Wolds had been 'added in our time to the cornlands of England'.[10]

Tennyson recorded the same process of improvement in the *Northern Farmer*, referring to Thorganby Warren:

Dubbut looäk at the waäste: theer warn't not feäd for a cow,
Nowt at all but bracken an' fuzz, an' looäk at it now,
Warn't worth nowt a haäcre an' now theer's ots o' feäd,
Fourscore yows upon it an' some on it doon in seäd. [11]

On the land itself, improvements such as selective cross-breeding of animals were combined with higher levels of investment. This led to a steadily increasing ratio of livestock to acreage. At the same time, increasing amounts of pasture land came under the plough, investment resulting in wheat yields rising from 20–24 bushels per acre in the 1790s to 28–32 bushels by the 1830s. National wheat yields did not reach this level until the 1860s.[12]

During the first thirty years of the 19th century, conditions were singularly favourable for farming investment. Rental levels on the Wolds compared to other areas of the county were low, an average rent of 8s in 1800 compared with £1 to £2 on the marsh and fenland. On warren farms the rent might be even lower; at Binbrook 6s an acre was paid in 1804. As a result, farming was sufficiently profitable for investment and improvement to continue, even at a time when other areas of the country were experiencing agricultural depression in consequence of the drop in agricultural prices experienced at the end of the war. Low levels of rent continued in the years following the Napoleonic Wars. Rental levels did not reach as high as the rest of Lincolnshire until the 1830s, by which time the transformation of agriculture was largely complete. This situation contrasts significantly with other areas of the country. In Lancashire, for instance, major agricultural investments on the fertile plains of west Lancashire seem to have taken place during the 1840s and 1850s while the agriculture of much of the rest of the county was not transformed until the third quarter of the century.[13]

High farming[14]

High farming is the term used to describe rising levels of agricultural productivity, developments in agricultural technology, and a very Victorian concept of 'improvement' during the middle years of the 19th century. High farming was epitomized by mixed farming using crop rotation in an intensive system with high inputs and high outputs. Not all areas of the country shared in this progress and not all farmers were swept along by the improving rhetoric, but it is clear that the farmers of the Lincolnshire Wolds, the larger-scale farmers in the area in particular, were regarded as exemplars of high farming. Such farming has left its mark on the built environment with the construction of extensive planned farmsteads in villages such as Kirmond Le Mire, Binbrook, Stainton Le Vale, and Stenigot along with associated estate housing in villages like Wold Newton.[15]

The information gathered on the state of farming at the time of tithe commutation provides clear evidence of the high standard of farming being practised in the 1830s and 1840s. At Beelsby, the land was 'as highly farmed as it can be', while at Kelstern the land was 'in an extraordinary state of high cultivation and the stock is stated to be the best in the country'. At Little Cawthorpe on the eastern edge of the Wolds, the assistant tithe commissioner went into considerable detail about recent improvements:

> An enclosure has just taken place under the general act and great improvements are in progress from that circumstance … one principal means of effecting these improvements is the 'chalking' of the strong soil, which is done at considerable expense by casting and spreading over the land about 100 tons of chalk per acre, when reduced to minute particles by exposure to the atmosphere. The melioration [*sic*] of the soil after this process is great and permanent.
>
> Bones are used with much advantage upon the dry limestone land. The cultivation has been indifferent prior to the present period and the value of the land is stated to have been only 20/– per acre including the Tithe; but it is evident that a considerable increase of value is about to take place.[16]

The Tithe Files also highlight how closely farming was integrated within the wider rural society. At times, there was undoubted strain between farming interests and the clergy. The major source of discontent was tithes. The tithes were the right of the clergy (or to be more accurate the tithe-receiving rectors and vicars), who fought hard to keep them as high as possible, while farmers regarded them as a tax which focused particularly on any improvements that they made to the value of their farms. The Tithe Commutation Act of 1836 and the subsequent wranglings over the value of tithes illustrate this well. The valuation for commutation purposes had to be a seven-year average of tithe payable before the act. All landowners and farmers tried to ensure

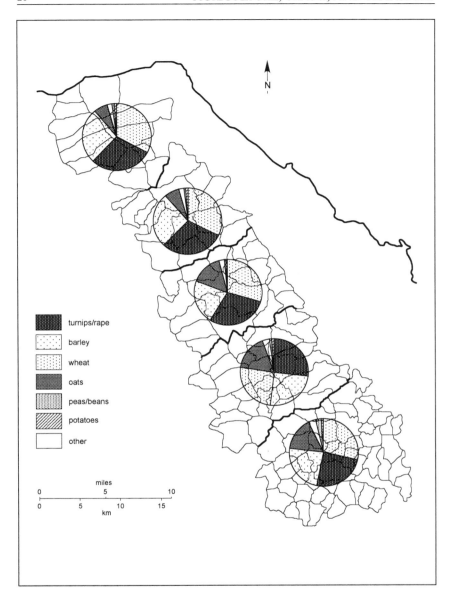

Fig. 6   Crop acreages on the Lincolnshire Wolds, 1867
Source: PRO. MAF 68/135

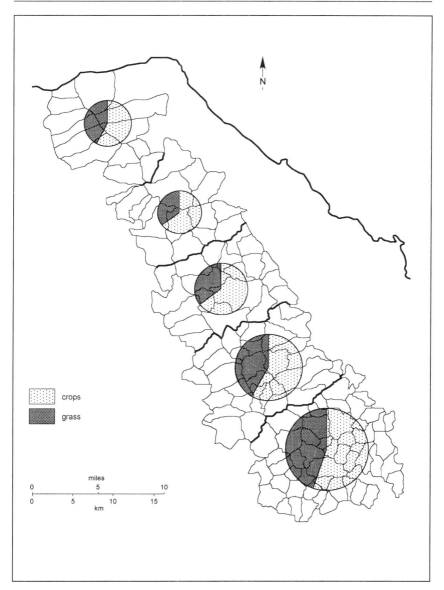

Fig. 7   Arable : grassland proportions on the Lincolnshire Wolds,
1867
Source: PRO. MAF 68/135

the seven-year period was taken when agriculture was in the doldrums, or they stood to pay out at high levels. As tithe figures were static once agreed, the rector or vicar might do very well if values were established at the top of the market, but farmers would suffer when agricultural incomes fell away. The farmers regarded improvements that had been made during the last 30 years as their own, while the clergy argued for a share of the enhanced value of the land.[17]

At North Ormsby, the value of the land was disputed between the tithe owner and the farmer. The tithe owner's valuer suggested that the land would produce four quarters of wheat per acre, seven to eight quarters of oats and five quarters of barley. The farmer, John Booth (980a) stated, 'Ormsby will not produce three quarters of wheat.' He continued, 'I recollect Ormsby when great part of it was warren.' Resentment was clearly felt against the payment of any kind of tithe: 'the land is poor on account of the tithes being taken in kind'. Booth produced a whole array of local farmers as witnesses to support his contention.[18]

At Wold Newton, the rector, Henry Milton, who lived at Market Weighton in Yorkshire, was unable to come to an agreement with Lord Yarborough's agent about the value of the tithes. Milton's surveyor had valued the parish at £720 per annum. Yarborough's agent did not dispute this figure but said, 'It is raised to that value by the high state of cultivation it is now found in ... [as a result] ...the Tithe owner ought not to receive any increased value of his tithes on that account.' Milton argued that the parish was worth £400 per annum in 1807, i.e. before the improvements in husbandry and that therefore £500 was a reasonable sum to ask. This was rejected. An increasingly desperate rector wrote to the bishop suggesting that the Assistant Tithe Commissioner had been 'tampered with'. He tried to get the bishop to speak against the Commutation Bill as it passed through the Lords, the implication here being that Lord Yarborough was using all his influence in favour of his farmers. The valuation was not finally agreed on until 1842.[19]

In the late 1830s, there was a similar battle over tithes at Beelsby. Here the complaints were religious as well as economic. The non-resident rector, George Wilkins wrote to Bishop Kaye: 'Every inhabitant … is a Wesleyan', while the people of Beelsby 'encouraged, nourished, caused and boarded all the itinerant preachers of the County giving up their barns for assembling the people.' Yet Wilkins did nothing to alter the situation, since his curate lived in Grimsby and only came to the village for one service each Sunday. The two principal farmers, John Sowerby and Thomas Coates, were united with their landlord John Adeane in opposing the rector. They still begrudged an earlier increase in tithe from £450 to £490: 'the increase was made on account of the quantity of land ploughed out from permanent grass – and we found from the increase of arable land we could not resist the increase – but we say now that we ought not to be charged for an improvement made in the parish since 1835.' The Assistant Commissioner suggested £576 before finally settling for £490, 'for the time being'.[20]

The tithe files illustrate both the tensions within rural society and also the progress being made on the farms. There is little doubt that, by the 1840s, farmers on the Wolds were well regarded by commentators as improvers and innovators. In 1843, Pusey stated, 'Lincolnshire affords a very high example of farming', while a series of articles in the *Journal of the Royal Agricultural Society* speak of the county's agriculture in glowing terms. Of the produce itself, by the 1830s livestock generally accounted for over 40 per cent of total returns of which sheep was the major animal and mutton the main product. Cattle were there 'to convert the straw into excellent dung'.[21]

By mid century the type of farming was well established, based on turnips and seeds as fodder for sheep and usually involving either a four-course rotation: (1) turnips, (2) barley, (3) seeds, (4) wheat; or a five-course rotation on the heavier soils of the eastern Wolds where barley had too strong a straw after turnips, damaging the subsequent clover: (1) turnips, (2) oats, (3) wheat, (4) seeds, (5) wheat. Similar rotations were maintained throughout the century.[22]

Oats were grown largely for horse fodder. Indeed, large numbers of horses were bred on the Wolds either for local use on the farms or for the Horncastle horse fairs. Surplus oats from the southern Wolds were also marketed at Boston.[23]

The area became well known for the quality of its sheep. As early as

1826, William Dawson of Withcall was producing heavy three-shear sheep. In 1847 Smith stated that the Lincoln–Leicester crosses produced on the Wolds ranked 'amongst the most valuable breeds for the purposes assigned to them, and are shown in great perfection at the Lincoln, Caistor, Boston &c, great spring fairs'. At Tathwell, Charles Chaplin crossed his Lincoln with Teeswater in an attempt to increase fleece weight.[24]

Sheep farming was considered to be central to the agricultural activity of the county to such an extent that the failure of Lincolnshire to be represented in the sheep classes at the Royal Agricultural Society Meeting in Leeds in 1861 was greeted with horror in the local press:

> Sheep breeding is the sheet anchor of the Lincolnshire farmer, and enables him to bear up against the vicissitudes of the season by relying more on sheep and wool than on his own crops. With men like Mr Torr of Aylesby and Mr Thos Kirkham of Biscathorpe, surely we need not be afraid to compete with any sheep breeders in England.[25]

Allowing for this minor setback, sheep were clearly a major factor in maintaining high levels of profitability through the period. In 1864, the sale catalogue of the Wyham and Cadeby estate was able to say (allowing for the estate agent's hyperbole): 'It is excellent wheat, turnip and barley land, and having so large a proportion of superior pasture land is peculiarly adapted for the production of lustre wool now so much in demand, and bearing such a high price in the manufacturing districts.'[26]

The cultivation of turnips remained crucial to the success of the mixed farming economy. In 1864, the *Louth and North Lincolnshire Advertiser* reported that, 'Due to the failure of the turnip crop, several hundreds of lambs are being slaughtered for market.'[27]

The Agricultural Crop and Livestock Returns provide a detailed picture of the agriculture of the area from 1866. As can be seen from Figures 6 and 7, mixed farming remained dominant. Across the whole area in 1867, wheat occupied the largest acreage, followed by turnips, barley and oats. The increased importance of wheat in the cropping system reflected the improvements in farming practices which enabled greater acreages of wheat, a more soil-demanding crop, to be grown than at the beginning of the century. Wheat at this time was the most profitable arable crop, and the ability of Wolds farmers to grow it successfully on a large scale enabled high levels of profitability to be achieved. Cropping patterns show greater consistency across the entire Wolds than at the beginning of the century. Only the south-central Wolds, where turnips and barley both slightly exceeded wheat acreages, varied from the norm. Crop acreages generally had increased from earlier in the century as agricultural practices improved. Fifty-nine percent of farmland was under crops, while 41 percent was under grass. The highest proportion of arable land was found on the higher central Wolds, with almost two-thirds of land under crops, while the lower, more dissected southern Wolds had only 55 percent of its land in arable cultivation. Sheep outnumbered cattle nearly fourteen fold (see Figure 8). Turnips, grown as fodder for the sheep, remained the lynchpin of an economy based very much on sheep.[28]

A detailed analysis in the *Journal of the Royal Agricultural Society* of three farms under the occupation of William Torr in 1869, at Rothwell, Riby, and Aylesby, provides us with a very clear picture of the type of farming carried out by the more substantial Wold tenant farmers. Torr occupied 2,280 acres, farming under a four-course system with both

Fig. 8   Livestock on the Lincolnshire Wolds, 1867

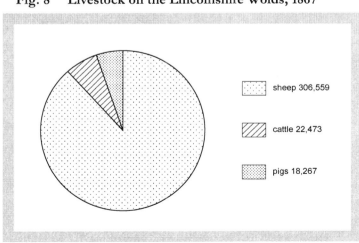

sheep 306,559

cattle 22,473

pigs 18,267

Source: PRO. MAF 68/135

cattle and sheep. The presence of a sizeable Shorthorn herd can be explained by his holding some 200 acres on the Humber Bank, an area which was equally well suited to cattle, unlike the chalk of the Wolds. His flock of sheep was famous throughout the country; indeed, as the *Journal* states:

> The letting-books of the last twenty years show how much, and how widely, Aylesby blood is appreciated. A very large number of rams have gone to Ireland, and a few even to Jamaica and St Helena; while near at home Mr. Torr numbers amongst his customers residents in Scotland, Wales and most of the English counties.[29]

We are thus presented with a picture of 'advanced ideas of good

Fig. 9   Leading Lincolnshire ram breeders, 1873–74
Left to right: **R. Howard, Mr Marshall, J. Cartwright, T. Casswell, E. Howard,J. Byron, H. Dudding, J. W. Kirkham, C. Clark, J. Harwood-Mackinder, Mr Hesseltine, W. Dudding, C. Clark, E. Pattinson, J. Turner, R. Wright, J.E. Casswell, E. Davy, J. Pears, J. Clark**
Photograph from the Museum of Lincolnshire Life

farming and successful breeding'. Whilst Torr may have been exceptionally able, his neighbour Henry Dudding was also one of the great sheep breeders of the 19th century (see Figure 9).

Clearly, the changes described in this chapter were quite remarkable. In less than 75 years (Young's original account was published in 1799), the Wolds had been transformed from an area regarded by contemporaries as an agricultural backwater to one that epitomized the virtues of Victorian High Farming. The pages of the *Journal of the Royal Agricultural Society of England* were filled with fulsome commentaries on aspects of Wold farming, and its leading lights were regarded very highly by 19th-century agriculturalists.[30]

Changes in agricultural technology had a considerable impact on the nature of rural life. The large Wold farms were considered to be exemplars of advanced cultivation throughout the period. For instance, the scythe rather than the sickle was used from an early date. By mid

Fig. 10   Burrell-Boyd 1856 engine ploughing at Louth
Steam ploughing engine demonstration held at Brackenborough
Source: *Illustrated London News*, Museum of Lincolnshire Life

century, machinery was being introduced progressively on to Wold farms. Clarke commented in 1852: 'Crosskill's clodcrusher, Hornsby drills, Garrett's horseshoe, the iron ploughs of Messrs Ransome, Howard, Barrett and Ashton; and other implements equally well known are common throughout the district' (see Figure 10, above).[31]

At the North Lincolnshire Agricultural Society Show in 1861, 'The company consist[ed] chiefly of farmers who took great interest in the trials of mowing machines, threshing machines and ploughs.' It was around this time that the gradual introduction of steam-powered cultivation took place. In 1864, the *Market Rasen Weekly Mail* commented:

> The harvest about Caistor is progressing rapidly. Reaping machines are fast coming into general use and the rapidity with which they travel round a 15 or 20 acre field of corn, and the men put it into stook after them, is astonishing. With a couple of these magic reapers and only a few extra hands, the harvest on a large farm is now accomplished in a few days with a routine and despatch at which our forefathers would have been perfectly amazed.[32]

Cornelius Stovin at Binbrook Hall (545 acres) began using the double-plough in 1871. In his diary he states:

> We shall not be locked up with ploughing work as we were last spring. We then hailed the double plough, for it opens our way for the summer work …. The reaper, the steam engine, and thrashing apparatus, the double plough, are Divine gifts to the agriculture of the 19th century … Farming has become a scientific as well as an industrial occupation.[33]

IRON FOUNDRY.

MARY SCAMAN.

Respectfully informs farmers and others in the neighbourhood that she has opened an iron foundry and is prepared to supply them with plough shares, ships, breasts, wheels, land rollers and all kinds of common castings at moderate prices delivered on their premises.

Source: LNLA, 14 January 1860

In the second half of the century, demand for agricultural implements had reached the point where even some of the relatively small villages had their own agricultural implement makers, as was the case in Beelsby in 1860, where Mary Scaman had an iron foundry.

83

Implements, &c.

Stand No. 108.—GOOD, GEORGE, West Street,
Great Grimsby.

Article 1011—Dog Cart (new) ; inv. and manuf. by Exhibitor.
Price £45.

1012—Ditto.   Price £37.

1013—Ditto.   Price £34 10s.

1014—Ditto.   Price £31 10s.

Stand No. 109—THOMPSON, ALEXANDER, Keelby,
Ulceby.

Article 1015—Broadcast Sowing Machine ; inv. by Brigham and
Bickerton, and manuf. by Exhibitor.   Price £12.

1016—Iron Double Plough ; inv. and manuf. by Exhibitor.   Price
£7 10s.

1017—Iron Double Plough, with paring shares ; inv. and manuf.
by Exhibitor.   Price £7 10s.

1018—Single Iron Plough, marked No. 1 ; inv. and manuf. by
Exhibitor.   Price £4.

1019—Single Iron Plough, marked No. 2 ; inv. and manuf. by
Exhibitor.   Price £4.

1020—One-horse Iron Plough ; inv. and manuf. by Exhibitor.
Price £3 7s 6d.

1021—One-horse Iron Grubber ; inv. and manuf. by Exhibitor.
Price £2 15s.

1022—Set of three flexible Iron Harrows ; manuf. by Exhibitor.
Price £4 10s.

1023—" Governor " Self Raker Reaping Machine ; inv. and manuf.
by R. Hornsby and Sons.   Price £29 8s.

1024—Collection of Water Cart Valves ; inv. and manuf. by Exhibitor.   Prices various.

1025—Jointed Drag Harrow, two parts, for three horses ; inv. and
manuf. by Exhibitor.   Price £3 10s.

1026—Set of 16 steel Drag Shares ; inv. and manuf. by Exhibitor.
Price per dozen, 10s.

1027—Improved Drill for Clover, Rye Grass, Wheat, and Barley ;
inv. and manuf. by Exhibitor.

1028—Combined Mower and Reaper, with iron frame ; inv. and
manuf. by Bamlett.   Price £27.

Stand No. 110.—TONG, EDMUND, West-gate, Lincoln.

Article 1029—Ten-row general purpose Drill, complete, fitted with
Chambers' Patent Barrel and Scrapers ; imp. and manuf. by Exhibitor.
Price £35.

**Fig. 11   Alexander Thompson entry at the
Lincolnshire Agricultural Show, 1871.**

Source: LAO. Stubbs, 1/16/3, 1871. Catalogue of entries.
Lincolnshire Agricultural Society

In Keelby, Alex Thompson seems to have been a very successful agricultural implement maker in the 1860s and 1870s. He had a stand at the North Lincolnshire Agricultural Society Annual Show from 1859 onwards and became a member of the Society in 1865, obviously considering this to be an excellent way of increasing sales, by becoming known throughout the north of the county. By the beginning of the 1870s, he had a very sizeable stand (see Figure 11, above). The society's annual subscription of 10s was not cheap (the average labourer at the time received between 12s – 20s a week), but it was worthwhile. In 1864 he won a prize of £1 for a Grubber and a further prize of 10s for a Drag Harrow and water cart valves; these feats were repeated in 1865 and 1866. It is worth pointing out that Alex Thompson was clearly operating on a larger scale than most village tradesmen, since he had a stand at all the annual shows throughout this period, including those as far south as Horncastle and Boston. More locally-orientated tradesmen tended only to have stands if the show was near to home. It was not worth their while to travel considerable distances.[34]

The rise in arable production depended on a simultaneous improvement in the ways in which cattle were kept. During the mid and late 19th century, the provision of large-scale and increasingly sophisticated methods of housing cattle was essential to ensure both quality livestock production and sustained soil fertility. Improvements were made to farm buildings as well as to implements. At Worlaby, on the northern Wolds, Astley Corbett of Elsham Hall built an impressive set of model farm buildings in 1873, flanked by four pairs of cottages for the labourers; Christopher Turnor did likewise at Kirmond Le Mire (see Figure 12); while at Stourton Hall Farm, Great Sturton, the Liveseys developed a late Victorian mechanized farm with engine house and chimney. It was laid out so that slurry from the crewyards could be pumped into a chamber from which methane gas was collected.[35]

However, progress and improvement was not a simple progression. The physical geography and climate of the area remained formidable opponents. In 1872, Charles Fieldsend, who farmed at Kirmond Le Mire, remarked to Cornelius Stovin of Binbrook Hall, 'we had not had a good crop of wheat since 1862 across our wolds'. Stovin, in his diary, continued: 'It was a very strong complaint to make against our cold

**Fig. 12   Farm buildings at Kirmond Le Mire: an impressive,
if now rather decaying, set of model farm buildings
constructed by Christopher Turnor**
Photo: Charles Rawding

hills. The winters destroy our plant and nothing has yet been discovered
to preserve the root against severe frosts.' The land in some ways
remained marginal for arable cultivation, although it is doubtful
whether many other areas of the country would have considered it in
such terms.[36]

The agricultural depression

From the second half of the 1870s, the profitability of agriculture
declined. A series of poor harvests caused by bad weather reduced
yields on farms. Previously, poor harvests had to some extent been
compensated for by high prices; however, prices remained static as a
consequence of cheap imports entering the country. In 1870, Britain
imported 28,827,000 hundredweight of wheat. By 1875, the figure
reached 42,673,000 and by 1880 had reached more than 44,000,000.

The combination of this flood of imports with a run of poor seasons put real pressure on farmers on the Wolds and had a traumatic effect on the farming communities.[37]

The years 1873–81 were unusually wet, resulting in late harvests and lower yields. On Mr Scorer's farm at Burwell, the last good harvest had been in 1874, when harvest began on 6 August and was finished on 4 September, yielding 5 quarters 1 bushel to the acre of wheat. By contrast, the harvest of 1879 did not start until 8 September and was not finished until 30 October, yielding only 2 quarters 4 bushels per acre. These lows seriously weakened the prosperity of the area.[38]

While the occasional bad season might be expected and could be accommodated, it was the continuing series of poor harvests combined with low prices which brought many farmers to their knees. By 1879, the *Louth and North Lincolnshire Advertiser* reported:

> The agricultural interest of the county is feeling to a very severe extent the bad years which have recently prevailed, and it is stated in official quarters that so many liquidations and compositions by farmers with their creditors as have been lately registered at the Lincoln County Court have not been known for a considerable number of years.[39]

The trends of the second half of the 1870s continued throughout the 1880s with prices falling from the beginning of the 1880s (see Table 1.1) caused mainly by the cheap foreign competition, at the same time as bad weather and relatively high labour costs were squeezing farmers

Table 1.1 Average corn prices at Horncastle

	1874–84	*1884–94*	*Decrease (%)*
Wheat	44s 9d	31s 5d	29.7
Barley	35s	29s	17.1
Oats	22s 4d	18s 10d	15.7

Source: BPP. 1895, XVI, p. 163

25   Beastall, *Agricultural revolution,* p. 168, *GFP,* 1 March 1861.
26   Brocklesby Archives. Miscellaneous Sale Document, Marris & Smith, Caistor, 18 July 1864.
27   *LNLA,* 1 October 1864.
28   PRO. MAF 68/135.
29   H. M. Jenkins, 'Aylesby, Riby and Rothwell farms near Grimsby, Lincolnshire in the occupation of Mr William Torr.', *JRASE,* 2nd ser., 5 (1869), pp. 415–42.
30   Jenkins, 'Aylesby', p. 416; Beastall, *Agricultural revolution,* pp. 167–8. For a discussion of agricultural revolution and transformation in a national context see Overton, *Agric. rev. in England.*
31   Clarke, *Farming of Lincs,* p. 83.
32   *LNLA,* 3 August 1861. *MRWM,* 20 August 1864.
33   *Journals of a Methodist farmer,* ed. J. Stovin, London, 1982, Foreword.
34   For a more detailed discussion of the Thompsons, see Chapter 5.
35   P. S. Barnwell and C. Giles, *English farmsteads 1750–1914*, Swindon, 1994, pp. 44–6. N. Pevsner and J. Harris, *The buildings of England. Lincolnshire*, London, 1989, pp. 334, 813.
36   Stovin, *Journals,* p. 47.
37   For an overview see R. Perron, *Agriculture in depression, 1870–1940*, Cambridge, 1995. A. Howkins, 'Peasants, servants and labourers: the marginal workforce in British agriculture *c.* 1870–1914', *AHR,* 42 (1994), p. 138.
38   BPP. 1895 XVI, pp. 158–9.
39   *LNLA,* 16 January 1879.
40   BPP. 1895 XVI, p. 157. BPP. 1895 XVI, p. 162.
41   For a more detailed discussion see J. H. Brown, 'Agriculture in Lincolnshire during the Great Depression. 1873–1896', PhD thesis, University of Manchester, 1978; J. Obelkevich, *Religion and rural society. South Lindsey 1825–1875*, Oxford, 1976, p. 15. Wool prices fell almost as sharply as wheat prices, declining by 50% between 1873 and 1896 (Perron, *Agriculture in depression, 1870–1940*, pp. 9–10). For an interesting and wide-ranging discussion of strategies developed during periods of agricultural depression, see J. Thirsk, *Alternative agriculture: a history,* Oxford, 1997. B. Afton, 'The great agricultural depression on the English chalklands: the Hampshire experience', *AHR,* 44 (1996), pp. 191–205.
42   BPP. 1895 XVI, p. 35.
43   R. Olney, *Rural society and county government in nineteenth century Lincolnshire,* Lincoln, 1979, p. 182. BPP. 1895 XVI, p. 129.
44   G. Boyce, *An early Victorian market town. Market Rasen in the eighteen*

fifities, Market Rasen, 1996, p. 31.

45   For a more detailed discussion of Horncastle, see P. Davey, *Lawless and immoral: policing a country town 1838–1857*, Leicester, 1983, pp.11–16.

46   Olney, *Rur. soc. and county govt*, pp. 14–15.

47   *LNLA*, 13 September 1884.

48   For Market Rasen, where two corn exchanges were built in the 1850s, see Boyce, *Market Rasen*, 1996, pp. 13–15. H. Martineau, 'A cameo of Caistor', *Lincolnshire Life*, January 1972, p. 39. *LRSM*, 31 March 1854, quoted in Boyce, *Market Rasen*, p. 16.

49   *LRSM*, 1 August 1856, cited in Boyce, *Market Rasen*, p. 31.

50   ibid.

51   Wright, *Lincs towns*, pp.73, 76, 79, 209. Squires, *West Lindsey*, p. 16.

52   R. Russell, *Barton on Humber in the 1850s*, Barton, 1984, p. 6.

53   R. Acton, 'The Market Rasen Canal, 1801–1980', *LHA*, 17, 1982, pp. 61–2; N. Pevsner & J. Harris, *The buildings of Lincolnshire*, London, 1989, p. 31; N. R. Wright, *Lincolnshire towns and industry, 1700–1914*, Lincoln, 1982, pp. 205, 207–8, 169, S. E. Squires, *West Lindsey yesterday: 1880–1980*, Gainsborough, 1983, p. 16. S. Squires and R. Russell, 'Claxby Ironstone Mine', *LHA*, 34 (1999), pp. 46–58.

54   Wright, *Lincs towns*, pp. 78, 212.

55   ibid., pp. 211–13.

56   PRO. IR18. 5338.

57   PRO. IR18. 4835, 5146. Squires, *West Lindsey*, p. 16.

58   The Marchioness of Londonderry, *Henry Chaplin, a memoir*, London, 1926, p. 12. Wright, *Lincs towns*, p. 186.

59   Davey, *Lawless and immoral*, p. 11; *White's 1856 Directory of Lincolnshire;* Wright, *Lincs towns*, p. 187. Acton, 'Rasen canal', p. 62.

60   Acton, 'Rasen canal', pp. 61–2. K. A. Frost, 'When trains ran to Spilsby', *Lincolnshire Life*, July 1968, p. 29.

61   *LRSM*, 23 October 1844. Stovin, *Journals*, pp. 106, 114.

62   Stovin, *Journals*, Foreword.

63   See Boyce, *Market Rasen*, pp. 31–6. Stovin, *Journals*, p. 7.

64   C. K. Rawding, *Binbrook 1900–1939*, Binbrook, 1991.

65   BPP. 1837–8 XX. D. Gregory, 'The friction of distance? Information circulation and the mails in early nineteenth century England', *Journal of Historical Geography*, 13 (1987), pp. 130–54.

2

THE ROLE OF THE LANDOWNER

In rural society, social and economic power was derived from the ownership of land. Landownership conferred not only great social prestige but, more importantly, wealth generated by rental income. This income provided a small group of people with a far greater level of material well being than that to which the rest of society could aspire and significant potential control over tenants and employees. The Wolds displayed many of the characteristics of 'landed' society. At the time of the 'New Domesday' survey of 1873, 28 per cent of Lincolnshire was in estates of over 10,000 acres compared to a national average of 24 per cent. However, the pattern of ownership was uneven. Small proprietors were concentrated in Holland and certain areas of Lindsey such as the Isle of Axholme and the coastal marshes, while part of Lindsey including the Wolds and most of Kesteven was held by the gentry and nobility. This chapter, along with the two subsequent chapters, provides an analysis of the development of society on the Wolds by looking at interactions between the various groups found in the area.[1]

The landowner and his estate

In 1877, Walford listed 223 heads of what he considered to be the 'County Families', that is to say, those landowning families with residences in Lincolnshire. His list was divided into three sections: the aristocracy (comprising 15 heads), the knights (13), and the rest. The leading landowners who lived on the Wolds were the earls of Yarborough, at Brocklesby Hall, the Tomlines at Riby, the Heneages of Hainton Hall, and the Boucheretts of Willingham Hall. The principal seat of the Chaplins was at Blankney, but they also owned land at Tathwell, while substantial absentee landlords included the Turnors of

Stoke Rochford in the south of the county and the Angersteins who were resident in London. The principal landholdings are shown in Table 2.1.[2]

Table 2.1 Landownership in Lincolnshire, 1883

Landowner	Place of residence	Acres	Rental (£)
The earl of Yarborough	Brocklesby	56,795	84,000
Henry Chaplin	Blankney	23,370	30,517
Christopher Turnor	Stoke Rochford	20,664	27,513
Wm Angerstein	Piccadilly	11,669	13,815
Edward Heneage	Hainton	10,761	15,527
George Tomline	Riby	8,439	11,534
H. R. Boucherett	North Willingham	5,834	7,823
The Revd W. Smyth	South Elkington	4,100	6,946
Champion Dymoke	Scrivelsby	3,605	4,955
Admiral d'Eyncourt	Tealby	3,504	6,200
C. Massingberd-Mundy	South Ormsby	3,358	4,784

Note: Acreage shown represents the total acreage of the landowner in Lincolnshire, including the Wolds.
Source: J. Bateman, *The great landowners of Great Britain and Ireland*, 1833

Figure 18 shows the concentration of land in the Wolds in the hands of certain families. The northern area of the Wolds was dominated by the 56,000 acres of the Brocklesby Estate; further south, the Angersteins had large holdings in three parishes, while the Heneages owned a block of land centred on Hainton Hall. The Chaplins of Blankney were the largest landowners in four parishes centred on Tathwell, while the Massingberd-Mundy's South Ormsby estate formed the fifth major landholding block on the Wolds.

In 1849 Pelham's Pillar (Figure 22) was built at a prominent point on the Wolds above Caistor, in direct line with the Mausoleum and Brocklesby House, to commemorate the planting of 12 million trees on the Yarborough estate between 1787 and 1823. Its impact today is reduced by the tall trees around it, yet it still provides an unparalleled

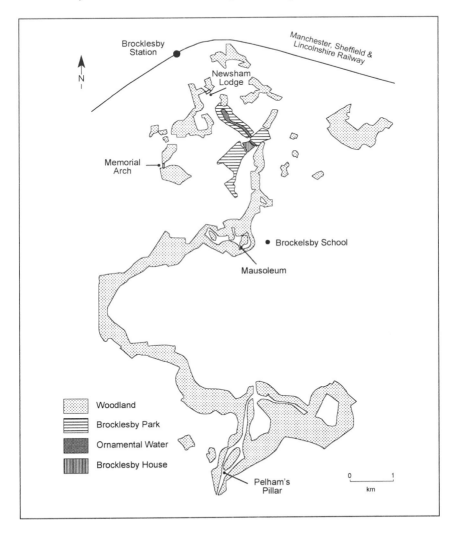

Fig. 20   The influence of Brocklesby

vantage point for viewing the Brocklesby estate. These landscape 'improvements' emphasized the central position and importance of the House. In the early 1820s, the second Lord Yarborough commissioned Wyatville to design a new house that would have exceeded the sixth

Fig. 21   The Pelham Mausoleum at Great Limber. Wyatt's masterpiece, completed by 1792, commemorated Sophie Aufrere who died as a young wife in 1786
Source: Charles Rawding

Fig. 22   Pelham's Pillar, 1848, built to commemorate the large-scale
plantings of timber on the Brocklesby estate
Source: Charles Rawding

**Fig. 23   Brocklesby Park Station. Butil 1848–9 in the estate style.
The 2nd earl was the chairman of the Manchester, Sheffield, and
Lincolnshire Railway**
Source: Charles Rawding

Duke of Devonshire's enlarged Chatsworth in size. The grand design
was never built, presumably on the grounds of expense, but instead
another wing was added to the west of the existing house connected by
a gallery.[8]

The second earl was a director of the Manchester, Sheffield, and
Lincolnshire Railway. As a result, the newly laid railway line between
Grimsby and Sheffield swept in a gentle arc avoiding Brocklesby Park,
rather than taking a more direct route. The earl arranged for Brocklesby
Park Station (Figure 23) to be built in the architectural style of his estate
just two miles from the Park and Hall. It was then linked directly to the
House with an impressive approach through Newsham Lodge (Figure
24). In 1864, the Memorial Arch (Figure 25) at the parish boundary
between Brocklesby and Kirmington added further to the grandeur and
glory of the Brocklesby estate, effectively producing a triumphal arch

**Fig. 24   Newsham Lodge, 1815, by Jeffry Wyatville,
on the north-west approach to the house**
Source: Charles Rawding

on one of the principal approaches to the house. It was built at a cost of over £2,000, paid for by 'tenants and friends'.[9]

A survey of the Yarborough estates in 1852 provides evidence of the importance of the country house, and the need to maintain an impressive presence in the landscape. The surveyor, Mr Parkinson, criticized the area around Brocklesby in the following way:

> Not any part of the Estate is more improvable. Deep underdraining for which there is good outfall and good management would cause these lands to be productive and to become of greater value to the Occupiers than they have heretofore been. Their contiguity to the Mansion is another great reason why they should be in a superior state of management.

Clearly it was felt that the area around the house needed to be a model of good husbandry if it was to reflect well on the estate.[10]

Fig. 25   The Memorial Arch, 1864
The inscription reads, 'To Charles Anderson Worsley, 2nd Earl of
Yarborough by his Tenants and Friends 1864'
Source: Charles Rawding

The Tennyson d'Eyncourt family provides a further example of how wealth was used to demonstrate social status. For most of the 18th century, the Tennysons were a family of reasonably well-off farmers. At the end of the century, George Tennyson, as a result of marrying an heiress and being a successful solicitor and shrewd businessman, was able to buy the Bayons Estate at Tealby. At that time the property had an 'unassuming Regency house'. In the Middle Ages, the property had been owned by an ancestor (related to George's mother), Francis, Lord Lovel and d'Eyncourt and there were traces of a medieval castle by the house. Through this ancestor, the family was able to trace its lineage ultimately to Edward III.[11]

In 1835 George died, his son Charles inherited and almost immediately added d'Eyncourt to his name as both a romantic gesture and a demonstration of the antiquity of his line. Along with the new name came a very impressive lineage, courtesy of J. B. Burke. Tennyson d'Eyncourt, as he now became known, also began to convert his house into a huge stone castle with gables and towers surrounded by battlements and a moat (see Figure 26). These changes were made to enhance the newly venerable Tennyson d'Eyncourt name. He added a

Fig. 26   Bayons Manor, rebuilt 1836–42:
the ultimate Victorian medieval Gothic castle
Source: Lincolnshire Library Service, Central Library, Lincoln

medieval dining hall, and the house was entirely reconstructed in the Gothic manner. Decorations were carved in the facade. Badges and coats-of-arms of the d'Eyncourts, Lovels, Beaumonts, Marmions, Greys, Plantagenets, Lancasters, Bardolphs, and others, through whom Charles claimed descent, were seen everywhere.[12]

Charles pulled down cottages. He created a fine park stocked with deer and sheep. A moat was dug and a lake stocked with curious aquatic birds. Charles created the impression of an ancient manor house, which had gradually evolved out of a feudal castle. He re-routed the drive, which meant the visitor was obliged to drive right round the Manor before crossing a wooden drawbridge, under a gate and portcullis (Figure 27). Such an arrangement made every visitor drive about half a mile further than was necessary. Finally, in the 1840s, he built an

Fig. 27   Bayons Manor: the barbican gateway. It was positioned on the north side of the house to ensure visitors had a full view of the house on their approach
Source: Charles Rawding

artificially ruined keep on a hill to the rear of the house within his newly created fortifications.[13]

From today's point of view, it would be easy to dismiss Tennyson d'Eyncourt as an eccentric; indeed, he was subject to some ridicule in the press at the time. However, his adoption of imposing ancestry and

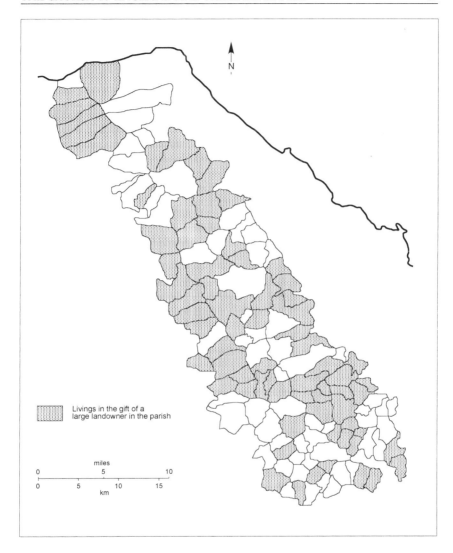

N

Livings in the gift of a
large landowner in the parish

miles
0   5   10
0   5   10   15
       km

Fig. 29   Church patronage on the Lincolnshire Wolds, 1855
Source: Post Office Directory of Lincolnshire 1855 and PRO. IR18

church, and needing a clergyman of whom they approved. Serious
reforms did not take place until well into the 20th century. As can be
seen on Figure 29, more than half of all livings on the Wolds were in the

gift of people with large landholdings in the parish. This system of patronage led to very clear links between the clergy and the gentry. The upper echelons of the clergy were often inseparable from the gentry and aristocracy. The Church was a favourite option, along with the army, for second sons. Having said this, some distinction needs to be made between the tithe-receiving rectors (who were not necessarily clerical) and vicars, and the lowlier curates who took most of the services and conducted the rites of passage in the parishes.

At the top of the Church hierarchy was the bishop. Bishop John Kaye (1827–53) was for a time resident at Willingham House, where he was accorded the same status as the Boucheretts. Indeed, on his departure, he received an address from the parishioners of North Willingham thanking him for his kindness while resident at Willingham House, and for the gift of church silver. This address was very similar in tone to the response reported in the *Stamford Mercury* to the arrival of the Boucheretts in the 1840s.[23]

Below the bishop in the ecclesiastical hierarchy were the rectors, whose large incomes were dependent on tithes. In many ways those rectors who were clergymen can be considered as members of the lower gentry. For instance, Robert Brackenbury, rector of Brocklesby, was the son of Sir John Brackenbury. They tended to marry into similar circles; the three daughters of George Holiwell, the rector of Swallow, married a colonial broker, a rector, and a 'gentleman'. Similarly, Isle Grant Overton, rector of Rothwell, married Martha Harneis, daughter of Theophilius Harneis of Hawerby Hall.[24]

The role of the clergy has to be seen within the overall context of rural society. They believed that men of superior rank and power were necessary to exercise authority over sinners. In a congregation, the parishioners could be observed and be instructed. As such, the parish church was a most conservative environment, with the clergy reinforcing the position of the landowners, both with their spiritual message and their social comment. For instance, the Revd Thomas Hardwicke Rawnsley, the rural dean of Bolingbroke, actively upheld the Willoughby de Eresby interest in the Spilsby area.[25]

Social divisions within the Church were very marked. The landowners received communion first and sat at the front, with the rest of society, according to their station, sitting behind them. Joseph Arch, the leader of the farmworkers' union, described this graphically. 'First up walked the squire to the communion rails; the farmers went up next, then up went the tradesmen, the shopkeeper, the wheelwright and the blacksmith; and then, the very last of all, went the poor agricultural labourers in their smock frocks. They walked up by themselves: nobody else knelt with them; it was as if they were unclean.'[26]

On occasion, farmers might buy pews or have them bought for them by their landowner. Thus, in 1846 Robert Raven (620 acres) of Little Limber Grange wrote to Bishop Kaye asking for permission for baptism and burial at Kirmington, even though technically his farm was in Brocklesby parish. His reason for asking was that 'Lord Yarborough expressed the wish that he [Raven's predecessor] should attend Kirmington Church, and provided a pew for that purpose.'[27]

The landowner and the parish church

Landowners not only had considerable control over the office of rector, they also created a clearly visible physical presence in their parish churches at the same time as they actively sought to encourage their workforce to attend those churches. Religious belief was often central to the lives of labouring men, and so influence over the religious environment by the ruling classes had an importance which can be easily missed today.

A survey of churches on the Wolds provides considerable evidence of the presence of the landowning classes within village communities, and gives a very clear picture of the social structure of rural north Lincolnshire. Four main groups of artefacts are found in the churches: memorial windows, monuments within the church, gravestones or tombs within the church, and elaborate tombs in the churchyard.[28]

The dominant criterion for 19th century display in a church was wealth. Only the wealthy could afford the various kinds of memorials, and only the wealthy could exercise the influence needed to see these monuments erected. Indeed, it is not until the First World War that monuments which incorporate the poorer classes are found in the churches to any obvious extent.

**Fig. 30   Swinhope: church and hall. St Helen's church is in the
foreground with Swinhope Hall and park in the background**
Source: Charles Rawding

The wealthy in rural society can be divided into four principal
categories, all of which are represented on church walls and in memorial
windows. First, at the apex of rural society stood the landowning
classes, below which were the tenantry, many of whom were very
wealthy men. Alongside these were the tithe-receiving clergy, ranging
from the younger sons of landed gentry, the so-called 'squarsons', down
to more humble clerics; a final grouping might be termed the
miscellaneous wealthy, such as local solicitors, agents for the large
estates, or other types of professionals and gentlemen.

In those parishes where there was a sizeable landowning presence,
there was a clear physical relationship between church and great house.
In many parishes with resident landowners, the churchyard can be
considered either as an appendage to the park, often with separate
access to the church for landowner and villager. The landowning
presence was equally visible within the parish church. The best example

of this is the small church of Swinhope St Helen, which can almost be regarded as the private chapel of the Alington family, since they owned all the parish, were patrons of the living, and also provided the rector, while the church itself was located within the park of Swinhope House (see Figure 30). Within the church there are a dozen memorial stones to various members of the family (see Figure 31) (six of the19th century, six of the 20th century) as well as both memorial windows and the family coat of arms placed above the entrance at the end of the nave. There are only two monuments in the church not directly concerned with the Alington family.

Fig. 31   Memorial to George Marmaduke Alington (1798–1890) in St Helen's church
Source: Charles Rawding

Nearby Cuxwold has a series of monuments to the Thorold family who lived at Cuxwold Hall. At Tealby, where the Tennyson d'Eyncourts lived at Bayons Manor, the landowning presence is also very impressive. Indeed, the chancel, with no fewer than nine recessed memorial stones and a stained glass window behind the altar bearing the various coats of arms relating to the Tennyson d'Eyncourt family, gives the appearance, almost, of being a private shrine. The chancel was enlarged in 1872 at the expense of Admiral Edwin Tennyson d'Eyncourt, specifically to accommodate the d'Eyncourt tombs and memorials.[29]

The church at Brocklesby, home of the earls of Yarborough, which one might expect to be a classic example of this type of parish church, is actually rather less imposing. One probable reason for the lack of 19th century display is the family Mausoleum, which rendered the church superfluous as a place of burial. Indeed, the general impression of Brocklesby church is of a restored nave that remains less grand than one might expect, and a preserved chancel, still containing the splendid monuments to earlier generations of the Pelham family.[30]

While many churches were extensively restored in the 19th century, churches in the parishes of the greater landowners tended to be better maintained overall, and therefore less in need of major repair work. As a result, more survives from earlier periods. For instance, the church of Langton St Peter and St Paul remains in its original condition as an outstanding example of a Classical Georgian church, having been built in 1725. Earlier monuments can be found at Scrivelsby St Benedict, commemorating the Dymokes from the mid 14th century onwards; along with four stained-glass windows to the family fitted during the 19th century when the church was extensively restored. At Spilsby St James, early Willoughby and Bertie monuments relate to the mansion of the Willoughby family at Eresby, while a superb series of family monuments to the Heneage family, some as early as the 15th century, can be found at Hainton.[31]

Of those churches heavily restored or rebuilt in the 19th century, Riby St Edmund provides an interesting insight into the structure of rural society and the ways in which the principal families of the parish created a visual presence in the church. The Tomlines rebuilt the church in the 1860s. The memorial window behind the altar commemorates George Tomline who paid for the rebuilding. In addition, the chancel contains three large coats of arms to the Tomline family, as well as two earlier family monuments. There is also a stained-glass window to Henry Dudding, 36 years a churchwarden, and a very grand 19th century memorial to the Reverend Parkinson, rector of Brocklesby. Apart from the landowners and the principal clergy, the final group of people to be represented in the church were the tenant farmers. At Riby, the Torr family have a stained-glass window dedicated to 'Five generations of Torr family. 1715–1875'. In addition, there are a whole series of 19th- and early 20th-century monuments to the Torrs.[32]

Churches in parishes where wealthy tenant farming families remained for a considerable length of time also tend to have more memorials than parishes which lacked continuity of occupation. To a large extent, this can be explained by the position of the tenant farmer within the rural community. Many were very rich men. The importance of such tenantry was reflected in the iconography of the church. The Torrs at Riby have already been mentioned. At Thorganby, the Bingham family is recorded in two memorial windows, the inscription below one of which reads, 'To the memory of the Bingham family so long connected with this Church and the parish of Thorganby'. Apart from these celebrations of the principal farming families (the practice continued into the 20th century with the Marris and Manby families), the decoration of Thorganby church is otherwise very simple. Great Limber shows a similar pattern to Riby. There are two memorial windows dedicated to the two principal tenant farmers of the parish, George Frankish and George Nelson, while the lectern was provided by George and John Nelson.[33]

In addition to memorials to the landowning and tenant farming classes, further groups within society can be identified as having sufficient wealth and influence to merit monuments within the church. The first group was the clergy, or to be more accurate, the wealthier rectors. For instance, at Thoresway, an otherwise very plain church, the only two monuments are to two Reverend Edward Coves (1776–1840 and 1802–1875). Similar monuments can be seen at Cuxwold, to the Reverend William Skynner, who was rector for 44 years, and at

Nettleton, where two stained-glass windows commemorate 19th century rectors, one of whom, Samuel Turner, paid the £1,800 needed to rebuild the church in the 1870s.

The second group can be less easily categorized, but might be termed miscellaneous men of wealth and influence. Into this category fall such people as the Marris family, wealthy solicitors who have three stained-glass windows at Nettleton, and Stephen Gibbons, Lord Yarborough's steward who is commemorated in a plaque in the Yarborough-owned parish of Swallow (see Figure 32).

Further evidence of the visual display of rural landowners and tenantry can often be seen in the churchyard. The graves of the poor were usually only given temporary markers, and there was distinct social segregation within the churchyard. The wealthy were buried on the south side of the church near the main door, while the poor were hidden away on the north side. At Riby, the Torr family graves form an impressive, if rather decaying, group, while there is a sizeable monument to the Sowerby family at Hatcliffe. At Swallow, the large tombs of the Farrows and their later relations, the Binghams, are concentrated around the church door. At Hawerby St Margaret, the presence of the Harneis family can still be seen in the overgrown graveyard, where the Harneises' plot is fenced in and contains impressive masonry. Likewise, the Marrises' grave at Nettleton now lies hidden and decaying behind more recent trees.[34]

If we now turn our attention to the parishes where landownership was more fragmented, some striking contrasts can be seen. Two large churches, Binbrook St Mary and St Gabriel and Ludford St Mary and St Peter, are remarkable for the absence of 19th-century monuments and the simplicity of their decoration. At Binbrook, there are only three artefacts which can be considered of the 19th century, a plaque commemorating William Burkinshaw, a farmer of 473 acres, who was churchwarden when the new church was built in the 1860s, and two stained-glass windows both relating to the first decade of the present century, but concerning people from principal families: Elizabeth Seer Johnson who lived at the Manor House and Albert Edward Alington, a younger son of the squire at neighbouring Swinhope. At Ludford, the simplicity of the church is even more pronounced. There is only one

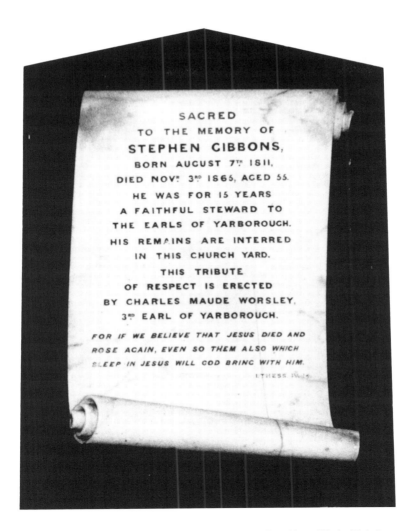

Fig. 32   Memorial to Stephen Gibbons, Swallow Holy Trinity
Source: Charles Rawding

stained glass window, which is not a memorial window, and there is only one monument, that being to Edward Alington Cooper who was the incumbent at the time of the rebuilding of the church in the 1860s, and who provided a large amount of the capital required.[35]

At Ludford, there were no major landowners with significant local influence, while at Binbrook, there were several large landowners in a large parish, but none was resident. Some of the parishes on estates also had churches with very simple interior decoration, as at Stainton Le Vale, Normanby Le Wold, Cabourne, and Irby. The crucial point here is that none of these parishes had a resident landowner nor a well-established, tenant-farming dynasty. It would appear that the crucial determinant of church iconography was place of residence of the wealthy.

The absence of church-supporting landowners might have a more dramatic effect on the parish concerned. In the case of Driby, half of the parish was sold in 1868 with the result that it became:

> owned and occupied by non-residents, who take no interest in church matters in the parish, give no subscriptions to church objects, usually engage non-conformist farmers and labourers, and change them so frequently that it is very difficult indeed to obtain any influence over them, while as far as they were able they have got rid of the church people who were in the parish before.[36]

The physical location and condition of the church might also prove a disadvantage in certain parishes. The church at Beelsby remained 'a melancholy picture of dilapidation and absolute ruin' until the 1870s when the first resident rector began an extensive improvement programme which was completed in 1890. Many of the churches on the Wolds were in a very poor condition. In 1835, Aswardby was 'no better than a barn', while Haugham was a 'mean barn-like church with no distinction'. In the 1840s Bonney found Hameringham a 'miserable remnant of a church', and Ashby Puerorum 'in a sad state'. Although many were later restored, Hameringham remained 'miserable' while Tetford and Mareham-on-the-Hill were 'lamentable'. At Goulceby, 'the present church ... is not only dilapidated, but inconveniently situated, being away from the people, whereas the Dissenting chapel is in the midst of the people'. At Walesby, the parishioners had a long walk up the hill to what is now known as the Ramblers' Church, the church in the village not being built until the beginning of the 20th century. In the case of Binbrook, the church was on a limb on the edge of the village, while the second Primitive chapel was built in a position dominating the Market Place.[37]

The revival of the Church of England

During the 19th century, there were significant changes in the nature of the Church of England. It moved from an almost exclusive relationship with the State to being one denomination, albeit the most powerful one. Through bodies such as the Ecclesiastical Commission and reformers such as Bishop Kaye, the Bishop of Lincoln (1827–1853), it became more active and responsive. The Church Building Act of 1818 and the establishment of what was to become the Incorporated Church Building Society (1826) resulted in a significant physical response as churches were built, rebuilt, or restored. During the second half of the century, over much of the Wolds, these reforms resulted in the progressive reduction of pluralism and absenteeism which had previously been the norm. In turn, these changes led to a more dynamic and committed local church. The most obvious physical evidence for these changes came in the form of building new churches and restoring or rebuilding existing structures. Over the period 1840–1882, no less than 663 churches in the Lincoln diocese were built, rebuilt, or restored, including 107 out of 132 on the Wolds (see Figure 33). Part of this revival was funded nationally or through the Incorporated Church Building Society, although much was funded by the local gentry, particularly the so-called 'squarsons', the tithe-receiving clergy often closely related to local landowning families. This was the case with the rebuilding of Raithby St Peter and Haugham which were funded by the Revd George Chaplin, a member of the Blankney family. At Haugham in 1840, Chaplin built a miniature replica of Louth church. Imitations of the grandeur of Louth's church were also provided on a small scale in churches at Raithby (1839) and Biscathorpe (1847). At times, achievements at the parish level were quite remarkable. The parish of Harrington had only 114 people in 1851, but led by the squire and the parson, it raised £1,000 towards a new church by the highly acclaimed Victorian architect, S. S. Teulon. At the same time, the rector acquired a new parsonage house by the same architect.[38]

No restoration
Barton
Brocklesby
Barnetby
Gt Limber
Keelby
Rothwell
Croxby
Normanby le Wold
Walesby
N Kelsey
Normsby
Wykham
N Willingham
Sotby
Biscathorpe
Cawkwell
Cackby Pockeave
S Thornby
Calceby
Cabourne
flot
Calcethorpe
E Wykeham
Langton le Partney
Boythby

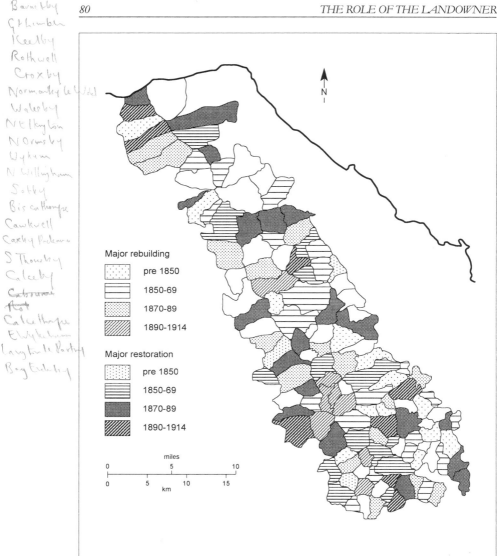

Major rebuilding
pre 1850
1850-69
1870-89
1890-1914

Major restoration
pre 1850
1850-69
1870-89
1890-1914

miles
0   5   10
0   5   10   15
km

Fig. 33   Church restoration and rebuilding in the 19th century
Source: various, including Pevsner 1989

The chapel and the landowner

Nationally, the gentry and aristocracy tended to support the established church; however, in Lincolnshire the ruling class was not always a bastion of support for the Established Church at the expense of the Methodists. On the Willoughbys' Ancaster estate, dissenters were not given tenancies. However, the earls of Yarborough were much more pragmatic. They not only had Methodist tenants, but also allowed Methodist chapels on their estate, where only a nominal rent was charged, as at Keelby where the Primitives were required to pay 1s a year for their chapel. Indeed, the Methodists of Limber were proud of building a chapel 'so near the residence of the noble earl'. At least one of the Tomlines was equally generous, as were the Eardleys at Nettleton, while the Heneages allowed chapels in three of the four parishes on their estate.[39]

In 1858, the *Stamford Mercury*, referring to the provision of schooling in Caistor, commented:

> that the Earl of Yarborough has kindly desired his name to be placed upon the committee ... his well known liberality on all subjects ... religious or otherwise, would have been a sufficient guarantee that the school would be established and conducted on the principle of dispensing its benefits to the most necessitous and in the widest circle.[40]

This liberal position was reinforced by additional donations to Wesleyan Day Schools. When G. F. Heneage, MP, made a gift of £20 for the construction of a new Wesleyan chapel on the Royal Dock in Grimsby, the paper at the time reported: 'although a true friend of the Church, [Heneage] has nevertheless always been a benefactor of Methodism and has ever displayed a spirit of liberality towards dissenters'. In this instance, his actions may have been influenced by an impending election![41]

By way of contrast, Heneage's brother Edward, ten years later, quite merrily dismantled the church tower at Sixhills (one of his estate villages) to provide stones for the roads! Edward Heneage regarded the church building as his own property to do with as he chose. He was sufficiently irreligious and self-confident to challenge the Church. Incidentally, he was proved right, despite the opprobrium accorded him by his neighbours and peers. When the vicar appealed to his superiors they did not back him up. At Nettleton, the principal landowner, Sir

Culling Eardley Smith, was more inclined towards the chapel, yet Methodism remained weak, perhaps as a consequence of the presence of a competent resident Church of England clergyman.[42]

The general approach of the gentry appears to have been followed by some tenant farmers. For instance, Charles Fieldsend at Kirmond Le Mire (1,287 acres) considered that his hired labourers were also 'engaged to go to Church', a fairly common practice on the Wolds. He would check their attendance at the Sunday morning service, but then in the evening would also go to the chapel and was, in fact, an active Binbrook Methodist. Until 1841, when a chapel was built in Great Limber, Mr George Nelson (1,400 acres) allowed one of his barns to be used for services, while farmers such as Cornelius Stovin were Methodist lay preachers.[43]

A further instance of the rather pragmatic approach to religion concerns several of the tenant farming families discussed earlier in relation to church iconography. The Coateses and the Fieldsends with memorials at Beelsby and Kirmond respectively, were Methodists. Christopher Coates is commemorated in Beelsby St Andrew, yet it was largely due to his generosity that a new chapel was built in Hatcliffe in 1838. Similarly, the memorial to Francis Sowerby in Hatcliffe church is to a man who left £1,000 to the Caistor and Laceby Methodist circuit in 1839.[44]

The social role of the landowner

The Yarboroughs, being among the wealthiest of Lincolnshire landowners, provide an excellent example of the role that the gentry and aristocracy fulfilled within society. For instance, the first earl founded the North Lincolnshire Agricultural Society in 1836. The Brocklesby Hunt was a major sporting feature across the north of the county. In addition the Yarboroughs were prominent in freemasonry, the second earl being Grand Master of the Province from 1849. The second earl was also involved in many public undertakings, such as the creation of the port of Gainsborough and the building of the Manchester, Sheffield and Lincolnshire Railway. He was chairman of the railway company and was lord lieutenant of the county.[45]

The country house was often the focus of a range of social activities which linked the villages of the estate and the wider local community with the landowner. In 1852, for instance,

> the children of Brocklesby Park School met at the school house (which was built by the Earl of Yarborough for the parishes of Brocklesby, Limber, Kirmington, Keelby and Habrough) and walked in procession through the pleasure grounds to Brocklesby Hall, where they were kindly received by the Countess and Lady Sophia Pelham; and shortly after her Ladyship had them taken through the principal rooms of the Hall, including the picture gallery, dining hall, etc., and then to the private grounds, dairy etc. They were next shown an immense number of toys, etc. for which they were to compete; each successful candidate received a prize. The servants' dining hall, which was tastefully decorated for the occasion, was laid out with a profusion of plum-cake and other requisites for a soiree.[46]

The local gentry were seen as the social figureheads of a village community and they were expected to take account of the welfare of their residents. Charitable donations were made by the gentry to worthy projects such as hospitals and schools (see Table 2.3). During the 1840s and 1850s, for instance, the Yarboroughs built a series of schools on

Table 2.3   Charitable donations by Lord Yarborough, 1874–5

Lincs County Hospital	Lincs Penitent Females Home
Midland Institute for the Blind	Market Rasen Dispensary and
Barton and North Lincs Ploughing	Cottage Hospital
Society	Horncastle Dispensary
Sheffield Public Hospital	Brocklesby Park School
Grimsby Benevolent Society	Schools at Ulceby, New Holland,
Grimsby Mechanics and Literary	Wootton, Cabourne, Horkstow
Institute	Keelby Foresters
Various clothing clubs, including	
Keelby, Kirmington, and Rothwell	

Source: LAO. YARB 5/2/2/14

their estate, while the Revd J. P. Parkinson, of East Ravendale, was instrumental in re-establishing the King Edward VI Grammar School, Louth, and Sir Culling Eardley Smith provided a school in Nettleton. In just one year, 1851, G. F. Heneage spent nearly £500 on subscriptions, supporting the South Wolds Hunt, the Caistor and Donington-on-Bain ploughing societies, and educational, medical, and other causes in the districts where he had property.[47]

The gentry organized funds for the establishment of reading rooms and literary institutes, provided gifts of food at various times in the year, and also money when needed, and gave awards for agricultural achievements and loyalty, through such bodies as the North Lincolnshire Agricultural Society. They also, on occasion, provided various social facilities or amenities. Yarborough, for instance, allowed annual Sunday School feasts and rural fetes of the Caistor Wesleyans to take place at Pelham's Pillar; Temperance gatherings took place at Thornton Abbey, which he also owned, while the Louth Cadet Corps were allowed to fish at Croxby Pond.[48]

A list of subscribers to Brocklesby Park School in 1860 provides an insight into the groups providing charity. Of the 25 subscribers, along with the Yarboroughs were 14 farmers, five clergymen and three professionals. During the 1860s and 1870s, William Smyth at South Elkington Hall held harvest suppers for his labourers, while his wife entertained 'about 70 children connected with the North and South Elkington day and Sunday schools (who) were treated with a holiday and kindly supplied with tea and plum cake from Elkington Hall'.[49]

Cottage building, pensions for old employees, roods of land for allotments, the provision of blankets, calicoes and coal for the poor, and the distribution of game at Christmas and the beginning of the shooting season were customary on estates like Hainton and Revesby.[50]

Charity might also be provided in less pleasant circumstances. The death of Robert Wilson, a farmer and blacksmith from Hatcliffe, resulted in Lord Yarborough sending £5 to his widow, son, and daughter, who had 'no other resource but parochial relief. The death occurred as a result of Wilson's cart being overturned in an incident involving the Brocklesby hounds.'[51]

On a more sentimental level, the pre-eminence of landowners in parish affairs was underlined by the way in which major events in their lives and those of their families were translated into objects of widespread joy or sympathy. A birth, the coming of age of an heir, his marriage, even a death, were all turned into matters of communal concern. At Tealby, the marriage of Miss d'Eyncourt in 1866 was celebrated with roast beef and plum pudding for all the estate's labourers at Bayons Manor, while mothers and children were provided with tea and plum cakes, and money was given to 40 widows and poor families. Formal gatherings often celebrated these kinds of events, yet however well intentioned these gatherings may have been, they inevitably carried with them an element of social conditioning – as such they were regarded with suspicion by certain of the more self-reliant farmers.[52]

However, the relationship between gentleman and villager might not always be smooth. In the mid 1840s, Tennyson d'Eyncourt received a petition from the villagers of Tealby asking for his support of the Post Office. Obviously some conflict had arisen, since in his response he agreed in principle, but would not support the present establishment. By the 1850s the relationship appears to have been much more friendly. The opening of the d'Eyncourt school was received with grateful praise and affection, while the extension of the school to form a rural institute in 1859, with reading room and a lecture series on scientific, literary and moral subjects, proved equally popular. However, beneath the velvet glove, the iron fist still remained, as illustrated by a notice from Bayons Manor severely reprimanding parents for the non-attendance of children at the school, particularly on a Sunday.[53]

The majority of the population appears to have accepted the prevailing social structure and one can well believe the *Lincolnshire, Rutland and Stamford Mercury* in 1844 when it stated:

> The arrival of Ayscoghe Boucherett and family at his ancestral mansion (Willingham House, near Market Rasen, the late residence of the respected Bishop of Lincoln) after an absence of eight years and upwards on the continent, has diffused universal joy through the village of Willingham, and in the district around, where their benevolence and affability have secured the esteem of all classes.[54]

In a different vein, the death of H. R. Boucherett in 1877 resulted in the tradesmen of Market Rasen putting up their shutters until the funeral: 'the deceased gentleman took in all improvements that could benefit the town, and the benevolence which prompted all his actions towards his poorer brethren will render it no easy task to fill the void his loss has left amongst us'.[55]

Similarly, the death of Charles Tennyson d'Eyncourt in 1861 was reported with a sense of common grief and loss. The procession from Bayons Manor to Tealby Church was headed by the family and local gentry, followed by:

> Mr Morrell [agent], his Son, and thirty Tenantry two and two, from Tealby, Usselby, Welton and Market Rasen. The children of the d'Eyncourt School headed by Mr Cochran. Foresters in the uniform of their order. The tradesmen and neighbours brought up the close and almost the whole body of villagers, men, women and children, accompanied the procession....
>
> The flag was drooping half-mast high on the tower of the beautiful house, that poem in stone which his genius has left ... the superb institute and school which his benevolence and taste had created and had intended to endow ... the children had a sad holiday today many groups of mothers and children were standing round the trunks of trees watching with sorrowful interest.[56]

These reports may be somewhat sycophantic, but nevertheless, underlying this, one suspects a considerable element of sincerity. Official celebrations were strongly encouraged as well. In Binbrook, for instance, the occasion of the Prince of Wales's marriage in 1859 was marked by processions and a tea for the children in the village. The report commented that the labourers were also remembered in such a manner as their several employers felt disposed.[57]

Justice and government

At the local level, the gentry acted as magistrates and Justices of the Peace, occupied positions as Guardians of the Poor Law Union, and were leading figures in the Volunteer Rifles. They chose the clergy where they held the living. A list of JPs for Lindsey in 1856 was comprised almost entirely of landowners, the principal clergy, and the larger tenant farmers (see Table 2.4).[58]

Table 2.4   Magistrates resident on the Lincolnshire Wolds, 1856

Kirton subdivision

G. M Alington	Swinhope	A. Boucherett	N. Willingham
C. T. d'Eyncourt	Tealby	G. H. T. d'Eyncourt	Tealby
Rev. W. Smyth	S. Elkington	T. G. Corbett	Elsham
G. F. Heneage	Hainton	H. R. Boucherett	N. Willingham
Rev. J. P. Parkinson	E. Ravendale	George Tomline	Riby
H. Smyth	S. Elkington	Rev. R. Brackenbury	Brocklesby
Rev. J. Browne	Gt Limber	Rev. J. T. Huntley	Binbrook

Louth & Spilsby subdivision

Rev. J. Alington	Candlesby	Sir E. Brackenbury	Skendelby
Fred'k Chaplin	Tathwell	Wm Elmhirst	W. Ashby
W. D. Field	Ulceby Grange	J. L. Ffytche	Thorpe Hall (S. Elkington)
G. F. Heneage	Hainton	Rev. T. Holloway	Spilsby
Rev. C. F. Massingberd	Ormsby	Rev. J. M. Lister	Muckton
John Wright	Spilsby	Rev. E. Rawnsley	Raithby Hall

Source: White's 1856 Directory of Lincolnshire

However, we should not assume that power was administered efficiently or by the most able of the ruling class. Cornelius Stovin, a leading Free Methodist, commented disparagingly on the Louth Board of Guardians in 1876:

You will perhaps be a little surprised to learn that the leading positions occupied by the members of our Louth Board of Guardians are most inefficiently filled. The chairman is too infirm and is unwise to cling to the office. Mr Wilson has confused and muddled his brain by drink and snuff. Dr Bell's abilities are of a very attenuated order. Rev Smith of Stewton fumbles over the medical allowances in a crude and blundering fashion. Colonel Smyth is a retiring, quiet, good natured gentleman without any gift of speech. Considerable hesitancy marks his oral performances. His brother rarely attempts to speak. Rev Vyner seldom comes and when present requires posting up by information and explanation. Rev Prettyman has the clearest judgement and most forcible utterance. Mr Smith and Hewson of Louth manifest some degree of business tact but little debating power or insight into law. There is not a single mind of commanding power to cut through the many difficulties which obstruct the course of business, hence very few persons can remain to the close in consequence of the lateness of the hour. The town of Louth seems almost barren of public men.[59]

This chapter has shown how the landowning classes had an influence over the society in which they lived which was far greater than is the case today. The concentration of such large landholdings on the Lincolnshire Wolds and the relative absence of smaller-scale landowners resulted in a distinctive picture emerging of life on the Wolds. In those parishes where the landowners held most of the land, their control reached into many aspects of economic, social, political and religious life, while they also created a distinctive landscape and architecture on their estates. In many cases, these landscapes have survived, however modified, while only in the few remaining estate villages do we find any semblance of the social influence so central to much of 19th century rural society. However, it was not until the First World War that the great sea-change took place in rural society which was to transform totally the social structure of rural life during the first half of the 20th century.[60]

Notes to Chapter 2

1   R. J. Olney, *Lincolnshire Politics, 1832–1885,* Oxford, 1973, pp. 12–13. A. Armstrong, *Farmworkers: a social and economic history. 1770–1980,* London, 1988, pp. 41.

2   M. Walford, *The county families of the United Kingdom,* 1877, pp. 1113–14.

3   R. J. Olney, *Rural society and county government in 19th century Lincolnshire,* Lincoln, 1979, p. 28. T. R. Leach and R. Pacey, *Lost Lincolnshire country houses,* Vol. 2, Burgh Le Marsh, 1992, pp. 4–22.

4   LAO. YARB 7/8; P. Horn, *The changing countryside in Victorian and Edwardian England and Wales,* London, 1984, p. 58.

5   See D. R. Mills, 'Country seats of the gentry', in *An historical atlas of Lincolnshire,* eds. S. Bennett and N. Bennett, Hull, 1993, p. 106.

6   T. R. Leach, *Lincolnshire country houses and their families. Part Two,* Dunholme, 1991, pp. 122–4.

7   D. Stroud, *Capability Brown,* Feltham, 1950, p. 145. For a more detailed description of the Mausoleum see *LRSM,* 16 October 1846. LAO. Misc. Dep. S. Shields, *Capability Brown at Brocklesby Park,* 1999. For a more detailed description of the architecture of the Brocklesby estate see N. Pevsner and J. Harris, *The buildings of Lincolnshire,* London, 2nd ed. 1989, pp. 187–92, 631. D. Linstrum, *Sir Jeffry Wyatville. Architect to the King,* Oxford, 1972, p. 231. R. Turner, *Capability Brown and the 18th century English landscape,* London, 1985, p. 167.

8   R. Arnold, *The farthest promised land,* Wellington, 1981, p. 141: H. A. Clemenson, *English country houses and landed estates,* London, 1982, pp. 76–7. Linstrum, *Wyatville,* p. 33. T. W. Beastall, *Agricultural revolution in Lincolnshire,* Lincoln, 1978, p. 218. For a more detailed architectural history of the house see Pevsner and Harris, *Buildings,* p. 188.

9   H. A. Fuller, 'Landownership and the Lindsey landscape', *Annals of the Association of American Geographers,* 1976, pp. 18–19.

10   LAO. YARB 5/1/20.

11   Much of the following information is taken from C. Tennyson, *Alfred Tennyson,* London, 1950; M. Girouard, *The Victorian country house,* Yale, 1971, p. 57. Tennyson was by no means exceptional in his efforts to recreate a medieval mansion. Indeed, Wyatville had undertaken an extensive remodelling of Windsor Castle for George IV in 1824. For an overview, see M. Girouard, *Return to Camelot,* Yale, 1981. For details of Tennyson and his associates, see pp. 69–76.

12   J. B. Burke, *A visitation of the seats and arms of the noblemen and gentlemen of Great Britain and Ireland,* London, 1855. Girouard, *Victorian house,* p. 57.

13   Tennyson, *Tennyson*, pp. 158–60. For a more detailed discussion see T.
      R. Leach and R. Pacey, *Lost Lincolnshire country houses. Bayons Manor*. Vol.
      3, Dunholme, 1993. M. Girouard, *Camelot*, 1981, p. 74.

14   *LRSM*, 2 February 1844; *White's Directory of Lincolnshire, 1872*.
      However, the Boucheretts had held land in North Willingham since
      the 17th century and may have been resident occasionally from the
      early 18th century; see J. Imray, 'The Boucheretts', *LH*, 2, 1955–6, pp.
      11–23. The point, of course, is not to disprove the antiquity of the
      Boucheretts, but to illustrate how popular perceptions of history may
      be very far from the truth. For a more general discussion of similar
      themes see *The invention of tradition*, ed. E. Hobsbawm, Cambridge,
      1983, particularly the essay on the British monarchy by D. Cannadine,
      'The context, meaning and performance of ritual: the British
      monarchy and the "invention of tradition", *c.* 1820–1977', pp. 101–64.

15   Brown's original plans are still in the possession of the family
      (personal communication with Mr J. Heneage); Pevsner and Harris,
      Buildings, p. 357.

16   Willson worked at Hainton from 1833 until his death and is buried in
      the parish churchyard. Pevsner and Harris, *Buildings*, pp. 83, 357. For a
      more detailed discussion of the buildings designed by Willson see
      leaflet produced for field visit by Society for Lincolnshire History and
      Archaeology, 'Notes for visit to Hainton, 6th September 1986'.
      Willson was employed across the Heneage estate building properties in
      parishes such as Brackenborough. See E. Bennett, *Brackenborough: the
      story of a manor*, Louth, 1995, p. 12.

17   R. F. Doris, 'Portraits in Stone', *Lincolnshire Life*, April 1978, pp. 27–9.
      H. Sharpe, 'For Hainton read Heneage', *Lincolnshire Life*, April 1978,
      pp. 22–6. For a detailed discussion of the Heneage family see T. R.
      Leach, *Houses and families*, vol. 2, pp. 167–86.

18   *LNLA*, 18 February 1860.

19   Fuller, *Lindsey landscape*, pp. 15–16. For a more general discussion see
      T. Williamson & E. Bellamy, *Property and landscape*, London, 1987, pp.
      125–9. For an overview of planned settlements see G. Darley, *Villages
      of vision*, London, 1975. A. Mitson and B. Cox, 'Victorian Estate
      Housing on the Yarborough Estate, Lincolnshire', *Rural History*, 1995
      (6), pp. 29–45.

20   Pevsner and Harris, *Buildings*, pp. 372, 547, 666, 742.

21   C. Wilson, 'Christopher Turnor: an agricultural improver', paper
      presented to the East Midlands Industrial Archaeology Conference, 24
      October 1987.

22   T. R. Leach, *Lost Lincs houses*, vol. 1, p. 15.

23 LAO. COR B5/4/126/1. Kaye was resident while building work took place at his palace at Riseholme.

24 Swallow Marriage Register, 2 March 1848. Swallow Marriage Register, 27 August 1850, Julia Holiwell to James Dignall; 2 March 1848, Ann Holiwell to Robert Brackenbury (rector of Brocklesby); 10 November 1857, Georgiana Holiwell to George Gordon. Thorganby Marriage Register, 16 October 1844. C. Phythian-Adams, *Rethinking English local history*, Leicester, 1987, p. 36.

25 R. J. Olney, *Rural society*, p. 53.

26 *Joseph Arch, the story of his life told by himself*, ed. the Countess of Warwick, London, 1898, p. 20.

27 LAO. COR B5/4/43/9. 31 March 1846.

28 See C. K. Rawding, 'The iconography of churches: a case study of landownership and power in 19th century north Lincolnshire', *Journal of Historical Geography*, 16, 1990, pp. 157–76.

29 See Tennyson, *Tennyson*, London, 1950 for a more detailed discussion.

30 For a more detailed description, see *Lincolnshire church notes made by William John Monson, 1828–1840*, ed. John, ninth lord Monson, Hereford, 1936, pp. 58–60.

31 Pevsner and Harris, *Buildings*, pp. 357, 426, 630, 679.

32 Henry Dudding lived at Riby Grange and farmed 630 acres. It was common for the principal farmers in the parish to be the churchwardens.

33 *LC.*, 5 January 1877. A memorial stone to the son of George Nelson can be seen on the Barton Street near Cadeby Hall. See D. Tyson, 'Memorial stones in an unusual place', *Lincolnshire Family History Society*, 9 (1998), pp. 150–3

34 T. Williamson and E. Bellamy, *Property and landscape*, London, 1987, pp. 179–80.

35 1881 CEB.

36 J. Obelkevich, *Religion and rural society*, Oxford, 1973, p. 163.

37 LAO. COR B5/4/8/2, 8 September 1837. Quoted in A. C. Sinclair, *A history of Beelsby*, London, 1947, pp. 77–80. Obelkevich, *Religion*, pp. 107–8. Dixon to Queen Anne's Bounty, 10 July 1872, QABF 1930, cited in Monson, *Church notes*, pp. 10, 177.

38 Pevsner and Harris, *Buildings*, p. 605, Beastall, *Agricultural revolution*, p. 228, Olney, *Rural society*, p. 121. *Bonney's Church notes*, ed. N. S. Harding, Lincoln, 1935, p. 120. F. Knight, *The nineteenth century church and English society*, Cambridge 1995, pp. ix–xi, 64–6. For an example of the role of the ICBS in the rebuilding of a parish church see C. Rawding, 'To the Glory of God ?', *L.H.A.*, 25, 1990. pp. 41–6.

39   *LRSM,* 16 July 1841. W. Leary, *Lincolnshire Methodism,* Buckingham, 1988, p. 35. G. Lester, *Grimsby Methodism and the Wesleys in Lincolnshire,* London, 1890, p. 119. Leary, *Lincs Methodism,* p. 68. Obelkevich, *Religion,* pp. 30–5, 199–200. *LRSM,* 26 November 1858.

40   R. C. Russell, *History of Schools and Education in Lindsey, Lincolnshire 1800–1902. Part I. Lindsey,*1965 , p. 35.

41   *LNLA,* 7 April 1860.

42   ibid., 3 September 1870 and succeeding correspondence. The vicar and Heneage proceeded to have a very lively argument through the pages of the paper until ultimately the vicar agreed to resign on condition that the church tower was rebuilt. The tower was finally rebuilt in 1875. The religious role of the Heneages is further complicated by the Catholic tradition within the family. The family were Catholic in the 17th and 18th centuries, and it was not until 1813 that G. R. Heneage became a member of the Church of England, apparently in order that he might serve as sheriff of the county. Lincolnshire History and Archaeology leaflet, 'Notes for visit to Hainton. Edward James Willson. Estate architect Hainton 1833–1854', p. 3. Nettleton WEA, *Aspects of life and work in Nettleton in the nineteenth century,* Nettleton, 1980, pp. 14–29 for a fuller discussion.

43   I am grateful to the late Mr Michael Sleight for this information that was related to him by John Fieldsend, the son of Charles Fieldsend. Lester, *Grimsby Methodism; Journals of a Methodist farmer,* ed. J. Stovin, London, 1982.

44   Lester, *Grimsby Methodism,* pp. 109, 119.

45   For a fuller description of the Brocklesby Hunt, see G. E. Collins, *History of the Brocklesby hounds, 1700–1901,* London, 1902; G. E. Collins, *Farming and fox hunting,* n.d. R. J. Olney, *Lincolnshire politics,* Oxford, 1973, p. 44.

46   Cited in R. C. Russell; *A History of Schools and Education in Lindsey, Lincolnshire 1800–1902. Part III. The Church of England and the provision of elementary education, Lindsey,* 1966, p. 81.

47   R. C. Russell, *A history of schools and education in Lindsey. Lincolnshire 1800–1902. Part I. The foundation and maintenance of schools for the poor,* Lindsey, 1965a; *Part II. Sunday schools in Lindsey – the 'miserable compromise' of the Sunday school.* Lindsey, 1965; *Part IV. Methodism and the provision of day schools,* Lindsey, 1966. *LNLA,* 18 March 1863. R. C. Russell, *A history of elementary schools and adult education in Nettleton and Caistor,* Nettleton, 1960.

48 Russell, *A history of elementary schools and adult education in Nettleton and Caistor*, p. 26 *et passim*. R. C. Russell, *The water drinkers in Lindsey*, Barton-on-Humber, 1987, p. 18 *et passim*. *LNLA*, 10 August 1861.

49 The three professionals were all employed at Brocklesby: a land agent, a surveyor, and a clerk; *Whites 1856 Directory*. I have been unable to find out anything concerning the remaining subscriber, Mrs Powell. *LNLA*, 11 October 1873; 18 August 1860.

50 T. W. Beastall, *Agricultural revolution*, p. 230.

51 *LNLA*, 27 February 1869.

52 P. Horn, *Changing countryside*, pp. 37–8. *LRSM*, 16 February 1866.

53 LAO. TDE H/40/53, mid 1840s undated. LAO.2 TDE H/57/2 & 7. *MRWM*, 15 January 1859, 22 January 1859. LAO.2 TDE H 57/3. LAO.2 TDE 57/5.

54 *LRSM*, 2 February 1844.

55 *LC,* 15 June 1877

56 *MRWM,* 3 August 1861.

57 *MRWM*, 28 March 1859.

58 Charles Chaplin of Blankney whilst sitting on the Bench is reported to have reprimanded a young lawyer from London: 'you are evidently a stranger in these parts or you would know that my word is law'. Marchioness of Londonderry, *Henry Chaplin: a memoir*, London, 1926, p. 11.

59 *Journals*, ed. J. Stovin, Foreword.

60 For a fuller discussion of the changing role of the aristocracy, see D. Cannadine, *The decline and fall of the British aristocracy*, Yale, 1990.

3
THE TENANT FARMER AND THE LANDLORD

The previous chapter looked at the influence of the landowners on the landscape and on society on the 19th-century Lincolnshire Wolds. In this chapter, the focus shifts to the role of the large-scale tenant farmers and to their relations with their landlords. This was a pivotal relationship in determining the direction in which 19th-century rural society developed on the Wolds. The chapter begins by looking at the principal economic relationship between tenant and landlord, agricultural rent, and the range of obligations and responsibilities which made up the overall system of 'tenant-right'. It then addresses issues which affected the management of the land and the running of the estates. Finally, it looks at the role of tenant farmers within the rural communities of the Wolds.

As we have already seen, farms were large on the Wolds. The high levels of investment required to effect the transformation that occurred during the early years of the 19th century could only be carried out by wealthy landowners and farmers. As early as 1813, Young was able to state:

> There is nothing in the state of property in Lincolnshire, that pleased me more than to find on the Wolds, and especially about Louth, men possessed of estates of three, four, five or even six or seven hundred [guineas] a year, and yet remaining farmers, occupying other farms hired, and some of them living on their own...such men are able to cultivate their land well.[1]

In 1852 Clarke reported, 'The whole of the improvements have been accomplished on a grand scale: the holdings are very large, there being scarcely a single farm under the size of 300 acres, many contain 800, 1000, 1500, and more acres.'[2]

Farms over 400 acres were common, particularly on the central and northern areas of the Wolds. On the Yarborough estate for instance, leaving aside farms less than 49 acres, some of which were attached to such activities as milling, gardening, and innkeeping, the average size of farms was 412 acres. In 1832–3, 26,384 acres of the Brocklesby estate were farmed by 46 tenants in holdings of over 300 acres. Of this acreage, 15,244 acres were held by only 20 tenants in farms of 600 acres or more. The fifteen largest tenant farmers on the Brocklesby estate held upwards of 675 acres each in the early 1830s, while William Dawson held the largest farm of all under Lord Willoughby d'Eresby at Withcall, comprising 2,655 acres. By the 1870s, the same farm was held by Richard Wilson who, in total, farmed 3,200 acres. In 1873, a meeting of local farmers held in Binbrook was attended by 57 farmers, who between them held over 38,000 acres of land.[3]

To discuss 'large' and 'small' farms in such terms is, in itself, a reflection of the distinctive nature of farming on the Lincolnshire Wolds, since farms of 400 acres were unusually large in national terms. Indeed, many commentators thought lower rents for large farms were inevitable since there were few tenants available with the capital to take on such farms. By the late 19th century, this led to questioning of the large farm, on the grounds that it was not necessarily the most productive, particularly when compared to smaller farms employing less labour.[4]

The tenant farmers on such farms had to be men with substantial amounts of capital, and as such formed a distinctive layer in society that in many ways acted as a substitute for the gentry in areas where absentee landlords owned the land. At the same time as they formed an important and influential group in society, they also operated within an overall framework which was largely determined by their landlords and by the prevailing economic conditions in agriculture.

Agricultural rent

The payment of rent by the tenant to the landlord was the single most important element in the economic relationship between the two groups in society. Rent levels were determined by a range of factors, the most significant of which was the general prosperity of agriculture at any given time. Rents were generally low at the beginning of the century, reflecting the extensive agriculture prevalent at the end of the 18th century, when most of the land was used for sheep walks and rabbit warrens, when farm productivity was low and profit margins were small. The development of mixed farming, when corn prices were at record levels during the Napoleonic wars, transformed the agricultural picture on the Wolds, significantly increasing both productivity and profitability. There appears to have been something of a time lag before landlords recognized the new-found profitability of mixed farming. Nationally, rent levels rose significantly during the Napoleonic wars before falling back during the 1820s and 1830s. This was not the case on the Wolds where low rents may well have been the result of a deliberate policy to encourage investment. The steward of the Yarborough estates in the 1830s, justifying a policy of low rents during the first thirty years of the century, said that 'the land wanted subdividing and bringing into cultivation, the expense of these improvements, to a certain extent fell upon the tenant, but they were suffered to remain at this low rent until such time as it was considered that they were fairly remunerated for their outlay'.[5]

In many ways, Lincolnshire was unique at this time; nowhere were rents so low and so transformed during the first forty years of the century. By 1833, the transformation of agriculture was regarded as sufficiently complete and the tenants to have been sufficiently remunerated for their investment that rentals on the Yarborough estate were increased from 10s to 12s an acre to between 20s and 27s an acre. This contrasts markedly with the national picture where rental levels rose from about 12s an acre in 1800 to over 20s an acre by 1815 before levelling off. Only from the 1830s did trends in payments on the Wolds reflect national patterns. Writing in 1851, Caird confirmed the change in agricultural fortunes and subsequent rent levels when commenting about the Yarborough Estate at Great Limber: 'Sixty years ago (i.e. 1790) four tenants renting four thousand acres of land at one hundred and twenty five pounds each or two and six pence an acre became bankrupt. The same land is now yielding its owners upwards of four thousand pounds a year paid by prosperous farmers.'[6]

Agriculture remained prosperous until the 1870s. Early fears that the repeal of the Corn Laws in 1846 would end the period of prosperity by opening up the British market to cheaper foreign imports proved unfounded. By the 1860s, rent for Wold farms on the Yarborough estate generally ranged between 25s and 30s per acre. The so-called 'Golden Age' of farming was probably extended by a decade, as a result of wars both on the continent and in America. Rentals rose rapidly, but farmers were still able to make money.

The 1843 Income Tax Returns provide us with a basis for calculating rent levels by parish. As can be seen from Figure 34, rental values were highest on the lower land of the southern Wolds and the Wold dip-slopes where most parishes had rental levels greater than 28s per acre, whereas significantly lower rental levels were found on the higher Wolds where rental levels of less than 22s an acre were more common.[7]

By the 1860s, reflecting the continuing prosperity of agriculture, rent levels on the Wolds had risen overall. Having said this, rent levels did not necessarily rise in a steady and continuous progression. At Irby, the rent level on 410 acres let to William Nainby fell from £550 in 1843 to £468 in 1850 and to £452 in 1852 for reasons which are not clear. On the other hand, at Croxby rental levels were increased from £664 for 561 acres in 1851 to £730 in 1854 and £820 in 1865. In this instance, the change of tenure from Richard Nainby to his son Charles seems to have prompted the reassessment, since rental levels had been static during the 1840s.[8]

Rental levels continued to rise until 1878. The upward trend in rent levels undeniably created conflict between landlord and tenant. Not surprisingly, conflicts and disputes seem to have increased during the middle years of the century as landlords, in the light of the increased profitability of Wold farming, sought to raise levels that were perhaps artificially low. From the viewpoint of the farmer, these increases were introduced at a time when corn prices were lower than they had been in the earlier years of the century. As such, moves to increase rents were not popular with the tenants. Cornelius Stovin was a typical example of such a tenant. He had progressively improved his run-down farm at Binbrook Hall, and experienced high levels of profitability as a result.

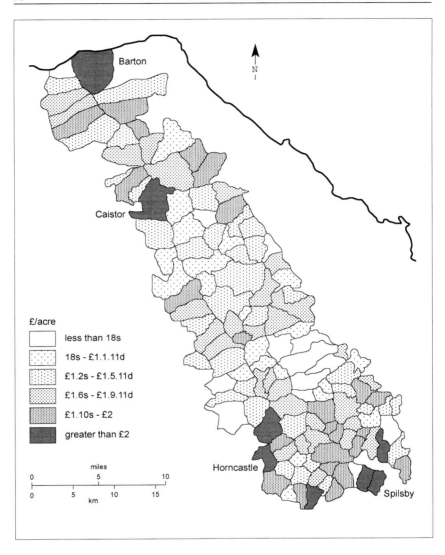

Fig. 34   Rental values on the Lincolnshire Wolds, 1843
Source: BPP. 1844, pp. 489–93

By the early 1870s, he was paying about 25s an acre. However, he was
aghast at some of the new rent levels being asked on the Wolds: 'Rents
continue to rise in all parts of this country. The Biscathorpe trustees are

raising Mr Kirkham's rent up to £2 or £2.2s an acre, Mr I. Sharpley of Calcethorpe positively declares we cannot live on our wold hills at two pounds per acre.' These figures were very high indeed compared to a national average of 25s to 29s an acre. Rents in Lincolnshire as a whole grew by between 15 and 24 percent in the period 1860–1878 and then declined by 20–29 percent over the next sixteen years.[9]

Rents effectively peaked at the point when agricultural profitability crashed in the 1870s, forcing many farmers to cut back on their expenditure, eat into their accumulated capital or, in many instances, petition for bankruptcy. 1874 was the last of the profitable harvests. Bad weather hit yields for the rest of the decade and for the first time, prices could not rise to compensate, because of cheap imports from abroad, particularly from North America. Tenants pressed for reductions in rent levels, which in turn reduced the standard of living of the landlord. Rent reductions tended to be greater in north Lincolnshire than in the south as most of the land was arable and the farms were larger. There were fewer options for altering the system of farming, or for introducing variations such as market gardening.[10]

At times of agricultural depression, landlords had little option but to assist tenants by reducing rents (see Table 3.1 and Figure 35). In most cases a compromise was reached, since the landlord had no desire to have large farms in hand, as he might have difficulty finding new tenants for them. In 1879, frequent reductions of rent were reported, usually in the order of 10 percent. Over the following 15 years,

Table 3.1. Rent reductions in north Lincolnshire

	% reduction in rent	*Years*
Lord Yarborough	33	1879–94
Edmund Turnor	29	1879–94
Edward Heneage	44	1879–98

Source: BPP. 1895. XVI p. 170, Brown (1976), p. 80.

Barkwith House,

Wragby,

1 February 1880.

Dear *Madam,*

    I am directed by your Landlord, Mr. TURNOR, to apprize you that in consequence of the now-existing depression in agriculture, and the unfavourable season of 1879, it is his intention to give a return upon the Rents payable at the ensuing Audit.

    The abatement to be made to you upon the Half-year's Rent due at *Michaelmas* last, will be *Seventeen Pounds 10/-* being at the rate of *12 ¾* per cent.

    This allowance has been arrived at by careful and impartial consideration of the quality and Rent of the Farm in your occupation.

        I am, dear Sir,

           Yours faithfully,

              E. Young Macvicar

                     Agent.

Half-year's Rent. £   137. 10. 0

Abatement . .   17. 10. 0

Amount Payable. £ 120. 0. 0

To Mrs *Clarke, Binbrook*

Please send me the Receipt for Property Tax as soon as paid.

Fig. 35   Letter concerning rent reductions on the Turnor estate: Macvicar to Clarke, 1880

Source: CP

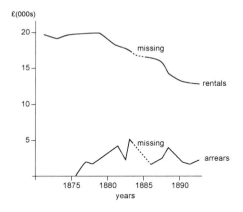

(a) The north Lincolnshire estate of the Turnors

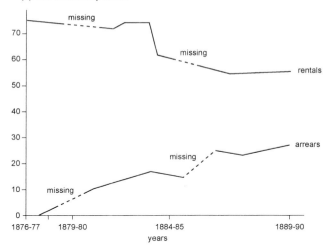

(b) The Brocklesby estate

Fig. 36   Rentals and arrears on Lincolnshire estates
Source: Brown 1976, pp. 82–3

reductions of between 30–50 percent were given, while the value of land fell by up to 75 percent.[11]

As well as rent reductions, landlords also gave rent remissions. Whereas a reduction was deemed to be permanent and was incorporated into the terms of a tenancy, a remission was considered as a temporary measure with 'normal' rental levels being resumed when a particular problem period was considered to be over. For this reason, remissions were preferred by landlords, as it meant that the 'official' rent level remained unaltered. Landlords were driven to extremes to obtain or retain tenants. Farms that were let by auction fetched only half of the previous rent. In most instances, landlords were faced not only with falling rentals, but also mounting arrears, as tenants faced up to financial crisis. Figure 36 shows the effect of the economic crisis on the Yarborough estate and the north Lincolnshire properties of the Turnors.[12]

Some of the more optimistic landlords embarked upon programmes of capital expenditure in an attempt to maintain existing returns or to retain tenants otherwise anxious to quit their holdings. However, by 1881 the rents on the Heneage estate had fallen to the levels of 1847 despite £100,000 having been spent on them on improvements in the intervening period. In 1886 Edward Heneage commented, 'I am afraid I shall lose some tenants of the larger farms even at reduced rents ... Landlords are in such a panic that they are letting at any price and giving thirty and fifty percent reductions ... farmers will not be practicable and reduce their own expenditure.'[13]

Over the period 1879–94, Yarborough spent £110,629 on improvements on his estate. Overall the area was noted for the excellent state of its farm buildings, which were significantly improved during the depression years, as the relative position of the tenant was so much stronger, and landlords had to accede to their demands in order to retain or acquire tenants. Such policies of investment were pursued by landed estates across the country, even though returns were often very low. In many cases, this investment was debt financed and ultimately led to increased land sales from the late 1870s.[14]

Nevertheless, the principal landowners could still count on a substantial rent roll, although some experienced severe financial difficulties. The Yarboroughs sold the whole of the parish of Wold Newton to William Wright in 1870 for over £100,000 to raise capital, and then sold the parish of Thorganby to the two sitting tenants, James Bingham (617 acres) and William Nainby (354 acres) in 1891. Indeed, in

1895, Yarborough was forced to sell his dog pack, retaining only the bitches. This decision perhaps had a greater social impact than a financial one, but it was highly indicative of the difficult financial conditions facing the family, reflecting a fall in rental income from £65,563 in 1880 to £52,083 by the turn of the century. Falling rent rolls were also reflected in falling land values, with the result that a heavily indebted landowner would find himself squeezed between a falling income and a mortgage company wanting security for its finance. This pattern was repeated across the arable counties of eastern England, as Barnes has shown in her study of Norfolk.[15]

The agricultural depression of the second half of the 1870s also led to a qualitative change in the relationship between tenants and landowners. In 1879, the obituary notice of Mr William Wright, of Wold Newton stated:

> he always supported his tenant F. Iles … he was one of the first of Lincolnshire landowners who said he would meet his tenants in regard to rent in a way which the landlords of the present day had a right to do, he said he felt bound to curtail his own expenses so that he might be in a position to meet his friends the tenants in a way that one man should meet another.

It is perhaps understandable that during the first period of sustained economic adversity of the century, landlord and tenant farmer should unite to enable both to survive the crisis, although the previous commitment to agricultural improvement was replaced by a desire for survival.[16]

As well as the changing economic conditions of the time, the policies of different landlords also had an influence on rent levels. Indeed, in 1852 Caird went so far as to suggest that, in Lincolnshire as a whole, 'rent varies more according to the character of the landlord than its [the land's] intrinsic qualities'. Generally speaking, larger landowners tended to charge lower rents than smaller landowners, while larger farms paid lower rents than smaller farms. Differences in rent levels between large and small farms seem to have been maintained right through the period. The sheer size of the larger Wold farms may also have had an impact on rent levels, since tenants capable of investing adequate capital into these farms were rare. As a result, landlords were often prepared to go to considerable lengths to accommodate tenants. These tendencies can be clearly seen on the Yarborough estate, where in the case of Keelby, the average rent level in 1860 was 45s 3d per acre. However, the three principal tenants of Lord Yarborough were paying much less than this (Table 3.2). The high average figure was undoubtedly distorted by the substantial number of small properties in this large village. In the 1880s, farms of over 400 acres on the Yarborough estate were paying an average of 19s 3d per acre, whilst farms smaller than 400 acres were paying 28s 9d per acre.[17]

Table 3.2   Tenants of Lord Yarborough in Keelby, 1862

	A	R	P	Rent	Cost/acre
Wm Frear Holgate (Keelby Grange)	531	3	32	664	25s
John Bower (Holly Farm)	222	3	21	285	25/4
John Towle (Church Farm)	113	0	22	150	26/6

Source: YARB 5/2/14/1

Tenant-right

The other central economic elements in the landlord–tenant relationship were the rights and obligations that made up part of the rental agreement and clearly defined the responsibility of each side with regard to the farm. In Lincolnshire, some landowners operated with formal leases for their tenants, but on the whole, leases were not the most common form of agreement. Instead, in Lincolnshire, the 'tenant-right' custom was operated, and tenancy frequently passed from father to son. 'Tenant-right' offered compensation to occupiers leaving their farms, with an independent assessment of the monies to be paid by the incoming tenant. As such, it provided financial protection and assurance, particularly when investment had resulted in the agricultural improvements of the first half of the 19th century. Investment in new methods, buildings, and in the land itself through draining, marling, and

extensive greenhouses maintained by a head gardener, producing exotic vegetables and fruits as well as flowers, both for the house and for the lady of the house to wear when hunting. In addition, they had a giant aviary filled with gold and silver pheasants. By the end of the century, however, such extravagances were largely replaced by a general tightening of belts as agricultural incomes went into free-fall.[55]

Tenant farmers might also be men of considerable standing locally, and even nationally. William Torr, who was both a landowner and a tenant farmer, occupied 2,280 acres at Riby and Aylesby. He was called upon to give expert evidence to the Select Committee on Agricultural Statistics in 1855, and from 1857 until his death in 1875 he was a member of the Council of the Royal Agricultural Society. The prowess of his farming merited a 27-page article in the journal of the society in 1869, while his death was marked by a six-page obituary written in glowing terms. The family was clearly an influential one, since his younger brother was M.P. for Liverpool. Torr was not the only local farmer to be an influential agriculturalist. William Frankish, a tenant of the Yarboroughs at Great Limber (460 acres), was a member of the Council of the Royal Agricultural Society from 1875, acting as Steward of Implements at the 1880 Show. Henry Dudding (Figure 38), who succeeded to Torr's farm in 1876, was considered the 'premier tenant farmer', and his annual sale of Lincoln sheep was second only to the Lincoln Show as a social event. Other Wold farmers had similar reputations; sheep from the Biscathorpe flock of the Kirkhams were in demand in South America.[56]

The tenant farming families can also be seen as a distinctive social group, often inter-marrying. The Stovins, for instance, were related to the Riggalls, the Sharpleys, and the Atkinsons (see Table 3.4). Altogether, the Sharpley family was said to farm about 12,000 acres in the Louth district of the Lincolnshire Wolds. The Coateses of Beelsby were related to the Bormans of Swallow, while the Marrises, who farmed over 800 acres at Great Limber, were related to most of their social equals for miles around.[57]

As well as running their farms, the larger farmers were also influential in local government and society, administering local charities, parish welfare schemes, and acting as Poor Law Guardians. In

Table 3.4   The Stovin family

Relation to Cornelius Stovin	Name	Location of farm	Acres (1871)
	Cornelius Stovin	Binbrook Hall	545
In-laws	Francis Riggall	Dexthorpe Fm nr Spilsby	400
Brother-in-law	John Atkinson	Grainthorpe Hall	Not given
Cousin	Croft Sharpley	Acthorpe	450
Wife's brother	Frank Riggall	Hackthorne	615
Others	Anthony Sharpley	Torrington	400
	Robert Riggall	Ulceby	870
	Isaac Sharpley Jn	Calcethorpe	420
	Isaac Sharpley	Boswell	1,209
	George Stovin	Sotby	1,200

Source: Stovin (1982) and 1871 Census Enumerators Books

Binbrook in the 1850s, three of the larger farmers, John Benn (179 acres – owner-occupier), Charles Fieldsend (708 acres at Kirmond Le Mire – tenant of Christopher Turnor), and Cornelius Stovin (545 acres – tenant of Beckett) were on a committee to establish a reading room. At a vestry meeting in the same parish in 1859, John Parr (farmer – 576 acres), and William Richardson (land surveyor and magistrate) were elected overseers, while John Fieldsend (farmer 380 acres), James Sumpter (schoolmaster), and John Maughan (master tailor) were elected as constables, and Thomas Wilson (farmer – 12 acres) and George Enderby (farmer – 145 acres) as surveyors of the highways. John Benn was elected as Guardian, while John Iles (farmer – 1300 acres) was Chairman. Some of these men were also highly influential in the non-conformist chapels in Binbrook.[58]

Tenant farmers such as Robert Martin of Asterby had considerable unofficial influence in local affairs. Such social leadership is clearly illustrated in a letter from the Rev. John Huntley, rector of Binbrook, to Christopher Turnor, one of the principal landowners, concerning Henry Clarke of the Manor House, whose death was 'a loss which can hardly be replaced by his successor, and it is without any disparagement to your Tenants to say of them that there is not the influence left to reconcile conflicting interests as was the case under Mr Clarke's management'.[59]

Clearly these tenant farmers were the social equals of the smaller landowners, living in substantial properties with a number of domestic servants (see Chapter 5). A perfect illustration of this point concerns J. Maunsell Richardson, formerly a tenant farmer at Great Limber, who took over the management of the Yarborough estate following the death of the third earl in 1875 (during the minority of the fourth earl). Indeed, he married the widowed countess in 1881.[60]

This chapter has shown the importance of the tenant farmer and of the landlord–tenant relationship on the Lincolnshire Wolds during the 19th century. In many ways, this chapter is very different from an equivalent chapter that might be written about other areas of the country. Farms were very large and farmers very wealthy. The Wolds, along with areas of Norfolk, Suffolk, and Cambridgeshire epitomized capitalist farming guided by scientific principle on largely arable land. The landlord–tenant relationship that developed can be seen as both a catalyst and a consequence of this system of farming. Significant contrasts can be drawn not only from further afield but also from within the county of Lincolnshire. Hall's study of farming life on the Lincolnshire Fens, for instance, details a totally different type of farming characterized by smaller holdings, less wealthy farmers, many of whom were dual occupationalists, and a more widespread owner-occupancy. In an area such as the Wolds, where landholdings were larger and tenancy common, an understanding of the dynamics of the landlord–tenant relationship is essential to an understanding of how society operated. It was these groups which effectively controlled rural society and wielded an influence which was very much a reflection of their economic power and social prestige. Subtle shifts in the relationship, often as a result of changing economic circumstances, could lead to wider-reaching ramifications and could spread down the social ladder to have a direct bearing on the economic well-being of the labouring classes.[61]

Notes to Chapter 3

1   A. Young, *General view of the county of Lincoln,* Newton Abbott, 1970, p. 21.
2   J. A. Clarke, *On the farming of Lincolnshire,* Prize Essay, London, 1852, pp. 76–7.
3   T. W. Beastall, *Agricultural revolution in Lincolnshire,* Lincoln, 1978, p. 180. R. J. Olney, *Lincolnshire politics 1832–1885,* Oxford, 1973, pp. 26–7; LAO. YARB 5 Surveys. Farm size does not necessarily correlate with acreage occupied by a single farmer. Many of the wealthier tenant farmers seem to have held several farms at a time. *LRSM,* 13 March 1874. R. J. Olney, *Rural Society and county government in nineteenth century Lincolnshire,* Lincoln, 1979, p. 56.
4   G. E. Mingay, *Rural life in Victorian England,* Stroud, 1990, p. 47, C. S. Orwin., 'The history of tenant-right', *The Estate Magazine,.* 39 (1939), pp. 198–202.
5   *LRSM,* 3 December 1830.
6   On agricultural rent see M. E. Turner, J. V. Beckett & B. Afton, *Agricultural rent in England 1690–1914,* Cambridge, 1997, ch. 8; Beastall *Agricultural revolution,* p. 182, J. Caird, *English Agriculture in 1850–1.* London, 1968, p. 193.
7   BPP. 1844. XXXII, pp. 489–93.
8   *LNLA,* 1 October 1864. Milligan-Manby Papers, Rental Agreements between Yarborough/Haigh and William Nainby, 1843, 1850, 1852. Milligan-Manby Papers, Rental Agreements between Yarborough and Richard and Charles Nainby, 1844, 1849, 1851, 1854, 1865.
9   *Journals of a Methodist farmer, 1871–1875,* ed. J. Stovin (1982), p. 10. D. B. Grigg, 'An index of regional change in English farming', *Transactions of the Institute of British Geographers,* 36 (1965), pp. 55–67. M. E. Turner, J. V. Beckett & B. Afton, *Agricultural rent in England 1690–1914,* Cambridge, 1997, p. 149.
10   BPP. 1895, XVI , p. 169.
11   J. H. Brown, 'Agriculture in Lincolnshire during the Great Depression. 1873–1896', PhD thesis, University of Manchester, 1978, p. 206.

12   P. Horn, *The changing countryside in Victorian and Edwardian England and Wales*, London, 1984, p. 31. Brown, *Agriculture in Lincolnshire*, 1978, p. 69.

13   BPP. 1895, XVI, pp. 135–6, 175;. H. A. Clemenson, *English country houses and landed estates,* London, 1982, p. 104. For the situation in Lancashire see G. Rogers, 'Lancashire and the great agricultural depression', *Northern History,* 22 (1986), pp. 250–68.

14   *LNLA,* 7 June 1879; Clemenson, *Landed Estates,* pp. 103–4. Horn, *Changing countryside,* p. 46. Turner *et al, Agricultural rent,* p. 265.

15   *LNLA,* 8 February 1879. P. Barnes, *Norfolk landowners since 1880,* Norwich, 1993.

16   Brown, *Agriculture in Lincolnshire,* p. 206.

17   For an overview see H. Levy, *Large and small holdings,* Cambridge, 1911.Caird quoted in J. A. Perkins, 'The prosperity of farming on the Lindsey uplands, 1813–1837', *Agricultural History Review,* 1976, p. 139.

18   See British Parliamentary Papers, *Report of the select committee on agricultural customs.* 1848 for a more detailed discussion of the Lincolnshire system and also British Parliamentary Papers, *Report from the Commissioners, inspectors and others on agricultural interests,* 1881, paras 6846–7234. British Parliamentary Papers, *Agricultural distress,* 1836, para 5852. D. B. Grigg, 'The development of tenant-right in South Lincolnshire', *L.H.,* 2 (1962), p. 42.

19   G. M. Williams, 'On the tenant's right to unexhausted improvements according to the custom of north Lincolnshire', *Journal of the Royal Agricultural Society of England,* 6 (1845), p. 45. This particular letter appears to have been circulated to other agricultural magazines. It appears in *The Farmer's Magazine* of July 1845, p. 77 and also in the *Journal of the Highland Agricultural Society*

20   P. Pusey , 'On the agricultural improvements of Lincolnshire', *JRASE,* 4 (1843), p. 299.

21   D. B. Grigg *Tenant-right,* p. 42. Mingay, in his introduction to J. Caird, *English Agriculture in 1850–1,* London, 1968, p. xxiv, suggests that tenant-right also gave rise to fraud and dispute – it often obliged the incoming tenant to sink too much capital into buying the improvements; he suggests that longer leases were needed. This was not the view at the time, at least not for Lincolnshire where, according to Clarke, *Farming of Lincolnshire,* p. 84, 'Tenant-right seems to be a thing better understood in this county than in many others'. J. R. Fisher, 'Landowners and English tenant-right. 1854–1852', *Agricultural History Review,* 31 (1983), pp. 15–25.

22   British Parliamentary Papers, *Agricultural customs,* 1848, p. 387.

23   Pusey, *Agricultural improvements*, p. 299.
24   Caird, *English agriculture*, pp. 117–18, 130–2, 194–6. *LRSM*, 25 July 1834.
25   *LRSM*, 25 July 1834.
26   Grigg, *Tenant-right*, p. 43. Orwin, *History tenant-right*, p. 199.
27   Beastall, *Agricultural revolution*, pp. 150–1.
28   LAO. YARB 5/1/20, 5/14/16, 5/1/20.
29   LAO. YARB 5/14/16.
30   Stovin, *Journals*, pp. 12, 140–1.
31   ibid., pp. 144, 188.
32   ibid., p. 145.
33   ibid., pp. 141, 148, 214.
34   LAO. YARB 9/19/1, Yarborough to Byron, 30 November 1846.
35   Olney. *Rural society*, p. 35.
36   *LRSM*, 26 November 1830.
37   J. Obelkevich, *Religion and rural society, South Lindsey, 1825–1875*, Oxford, 1976, p. 33. *Victoria County History of Lincolnshire*, London, 1906, p. 406. There are several different versions of this story – see also S. Sidney, *Railways and agriculture in North Lincolnshire*, Pickering, 1848, p. 80; G. E. Collins, *History of the Brocklesby hounds. 1700–1901*, London, 1902, p. 307; *Farmer's Magazine*, July 1849, p. 5.
38   Milligan-Manby papers. Letter from Yarborough to Stephen Gibbons, 15 March 1856.
39   *LRSM*, 25 September 1846.
40   Olney, *Lincolnshire politics*, p. 183.
41   Caird, *English Agriculture*, p. 25.
42   ibid., pp. 97–9, 196.
43   Stovin, *Journals*, p. 12.
44   ibid., pp. 47–8
45   ibid., p. 48.
46   Horn, *Changing countryside*, pp. 41–3
47   *LC*, 19 October 1877. *MRWM*, 8 July 1865.
48   Milligan-Manby Papers. Letter from J. H. Adeane to Richard Nainby, 9   September 1853.
49   *MRWM*, 4 July 1863.
50   See Collins, *Brocklesby hounds*, for a detailed history. Collins delimited the boundaries of the hunt as the River Trent to the west, the Humber to the north, the North Sea to the east and the line from Gainsborough to Louth to the south; all together an area some 25 miles by 45 miles. The pre-eminence of the Brocklesby pack, particularly during the early part of the century, undoubtedly enhanced

the standing of the Yarboroughs nationally as well as locally; see E. W. Bovill, *The England of Nimrod and Surtees 1815–1854,* Oxford, 1959, ch. 9.

51 Olney, *Rural Society,* p. 35. Beastall, *Agricultural revolution,* p. 154.

52 Obelkevich, *Religion,* pp. 26–7. Stovin, *Journals,* p. 175.

53 *LRSM,* 15 July 1830. J. A. Perkins, 'Tenure, tenant-right and agricultural progress in Lindsey, 1750–1850', *AHR,* 23 (1975), p. 9. Obelkevich, *Religion,* p. 33.

54 LAO. YARB 5/14/8, Estimate for a wold farm 1835–6. Olney, *Rural Society,* pp. 56, 59. Olney, *Lincolnshire politics,* pp. 39–40. Clemenson, *Landed estates,* pp. 103–4.

55 For a more detailed discussion see C. K. Rawding, *Binbrook in the 19th century,* Binbrook, 1989, p. 19. Horn, *Changing countryside,* p. 76.

56 H. M. Jenkins, 'Aylesby, Riby and Rothwell farms near Grimsby, Lincolnshire in the occupation of Mr William Torr', *JRASE,* 2nd ser., 5 (1869), pp. 415–42. 'William Torr: In memoriam. A compilation from many sources', *JRASE,* 2nd ser., 11 (1875), pp. 303–9. W. Frankish, 'Report of the Steward of Implements', *JRASE,* 2nd ser., 16 (1880), pp. 177–94.

57 R. C. Russell, *The revolt of the field in Lincolnshire,* Lincoln, 1956, p. 138 quoting *LRSM,* 28 October 1882. Swallow Marriage Register 18 October 1836. Olney, *Rural society,* p. 33, 55.

58 *LNLA,* 23 April 1860, 2 April 1859. For a more detailed discussion see C. K. Rawding, *Binbrook in the 19th century,* Binbrook, 1989, ch. 7.

59 Obelkevich, *Religion,* p. 55. CP, John Thomas Huntley to Christopher Turnor, 27 February 1867.

60 *Victoria County History of Lincolnshire,* vol. II, London (1906), p. 406. Quoted in Olney, *Rural society,* p. 35. Collins, *Brocklesby hounds,* pp. 215–16.

61 A. Hall, 'Fenland worker-peasants. The economy of smallholders at Rippingale, Lincolnshire, 1791–1871', *AHR,* Suppl. ser., 1, 1992.

4
THE LABOURER IN SOCIETY

The previous two chapters have looked at the role of the landowner and the tenant farmer within rural society. We now turn our attention to the agricultural workforce, as it was this group which was numerically the most important yet economically, politically, and socially the least influential throughout the century. Contemporary writing on the agricultural labourer is conspicuous by its absence. Indeed, only two voices speak out for the labourer during the century: William Cobbett, who wrote *Rural Rides* and entered parliament in 1832 at the age of 70, and Joseph Arch, who led the first trade union and himself became an MP in 1885. Although, compared to those of the farmer and landowner, the voice of the labourer was seldom heard, this is not to suggest that the agricultural workforce did not exert influence on specific events, nor that we should simply caricature them as downtrodden 'Hodge'-like rural simpletons at the beck and call of their overweening masters. Several major events stand out during the century, when the agricultural workforce discovered a collective voice. These were the 'Captain Swing' unrest of the 1830s, the 'Revolt of the Field' of the 1870s, the growth of agricultural trades unions, the success of non-conformity, and ultimately the mass emigrations in search of a better life in the colonies. Indeed, rural protest ran as a thread through much of English society throughout the 19th century. The most publicized episodes were merely the most obvious manifestations of this protest. None of these events took place in a vacuum, and the workforce needs to be understood both collectively and individually.[1]

This chapter begins by looking at the nature of the agricultural workforce, before assessing the economic relationship between the agricultural labourer and his employer, the farmer. It then looks at the

sometimes ambivalent relationship with the landowner, and finally at
the nature of the law and its implications for the labourer.

Fig. 39   Richard Aves, shepherd at Riby.
Photo, taken around 1910, of the shepherd at Riby 'since 1886'
Source: Museum of Lincolnshire Life

The agricultural workforce

Farm work on the Lincolnshire Wolds can perhaps best be categorized according to the conditions of employment. There was clear stratification amongst the farm labour force. At the top was the bailiff or foreman, below him would be either the shepherd or the head waggoner. This would depend on the relative importance of sheep on the farm (Figure 39). Below them were the rest of the labour force, each holding his own rank in the hierarchy. This hierarchy was generally very rigid. A head waggoner on the Wolds in the early part of this century recollects:

> I was the head man then .... And when we went to plough, I took the lead, and they'd do the same amount o' rounds as I did, but they musn't come in front o' me. No. It was discipline. And they wouldn' put a (horse) collar on in front o' me, nor yit a helter (halter) on. Because I'd gone through the same routine. The waggoner would do everything first, then the second chap, then the third chap.[2]

Each group within the hierarchy would be paid accordingly (see Table 4.1).

Table 4.1 Weekly wage rates on the Wolds, 1875

Foreman	27s
Confined men	18s
Shepherd	10s
Boy	8s 1½d

Source: Stovin, 1982, pp. 179, 193

Confined men

Confined men were those men with year-long employment, whether this involved living-in on the farm, in a tied cottage on the farm site, or elsewhere. Confined men had the most secure employment. They included all the key men on the farm: foreman, shepherd, garthman (who looked after the animals in the crewyard), waggoner, and so on. Often they would be housed in cottages on the farm. Where they were

Table 4.4   Witnesses to the 1867 Commission on the Employment of
Children, Young Persons and Women in Agriculture [Lincolnshire
Wolds]

Occupation	Number
Lincs Chamber of Agriculture	(1 full-page petition)
Large farmer	19
Child	9
Clergyman	6
Labourer	5
Labourer's wife	5
Relieving officer	2
Landowner	3
Doctor	1
Innkeeper	1
Schoolmaster	1
Gangmaster	1

Source: BPP. 1867

The practice was widespread and the gangs were a considerable
cause for concern to Victorian moralists and reformers. The 1867
Parliamentary Commission on the Employment of Children, Young
Persons and Women in Agriculture details the horrors of this particular
system of employment. Although an analysis of the people from the
Lincolnshire Wolds giving evidence (see Table 4.4) clearly shows the
sort of bias built into the 'fact finding', with the 'ruling classes' within
society providing much more evidence than any other group. For
instance, the Rev. J. G. Overton of Rothwell epitomized the Church's
thinking on the issue:

> I am certain that the only way to strike at the evils of field work is to
> forbid all female labour in the fields. First, I'm against all girls
> working, because they never make respectable servants afterwards.
> Then I object to mothers going, because they ought to look after
> their children. But for all women it's nasty, wet and demoralising
> work. Of course, I make an exception for hay and corn harvest.[15]

Similar sentiments were expressed by the vicar of Ludford. There
was considerable opposition to gangs from the 'respectable' classes.

The employing classes, however, had a different view of the gang system and of the role of women and children generally. The Lincolnshire Chamber of Agriculture did not want any restriction on the hours of work of women and children, nor the distance that they might walk to and from work. For children, they wished to see some form of elementary education and to ensure that the minimum age for children working in the fields be set at eight for boys and thirteen for girls. From a moral angle, it was important that: 'no unmarried woman under the age of 21 be employed in any mixed gang.'[16]

The gang system was not simply an unavoidable consequence of labour shortage, it was a very effective, cheap way of organizing casual labour for jobs such as weeding, picking up stones, and harvesting. 'Large farmers employ gangs here, small farmers look out for labourers with large families and employ their children.'[17]

For example, one gang, under a man named Neale, worked exclusively for John Iles at Binbrook Hill. Iles paid Neale, not the children. The work was done by contract, for as a neighbouring farmer, Higgins at Claxby, confirmed, 'weeding and taking up and storing of root crops are best done – that is more cheaply and with less trouble to the farmer – by boys and girls under a man who contracts by the acre or ton, and himself engages the children'.[18]

The Irish and the gypsies

In terms of the agricultural labour force, one further group needs mentioning, although strictly speaking they had little permanent impact on the area. This group comprised the Irish and the gypsies, itinerant labourers who seem to have returned to certain farms each year. The first major influx of Irish appears to have been in the 1820s. In many cases, Lincolnshire would form part of a circuit which might include:

Cheshire/Lancs	hay harvest
Derbys/Salop/N. Notts	late hay harvest/early corn harvest
Fens/Lincs/Yorks/Sstaffs/Warwk	corn harvest
Cheshire/Lancs	potato harvest

This would be followed by a return to Ireland in time for the potato harvest, and with the cash in hand to pay the rent in November.[19]

In some parts of the Wolds and Fens, the supply of Irish labour appears to have been critical at times of peak labour demand. Edward Gulson, the Assistant Poor Law Commissioner, reported in 1837 that 'were it not for the periodical visits of the Irish labourers who resort here in great numbers, the harvest could not be housed in Autumn. The amount of work done by the Irish during the harvest in this district far exceeds that which is performed in most of the agricultural districts of England.'[20]

The Irish appear to have been considered fairly respectable, although this did not prevent their suffering considerable harassment when there was a 'light' harvest and they were deemed to be taking work from local labourers. In common with many casual labourers on outlying farms, the Irish often slept in barns where they were working. Their position at the bottom of the labouring hierarchy was reflected in their wages. In 1867 Irish wages were 60–70 percent of the native rate.[21]

Apart from the Irish, migrant workers might be attracted to Lincolnshire from other counties on account of the high wages. Certainly there were complaints about workers moving from low-wage counties, but it is more difficult to ascertain how many moved, as these people had a much lower profile than the well-publicized Irish.[22]

During the second half of the century, the main sources of employment for the Irish, particularly reaping, were reduced, as farmers began to introduce reaping machines. Nevertheless, these itinerant workers helped to solve problems of labour shortage during periods of peak demand. In the case of the Irish, the numbers that came over tended to depend on the amount of work available the preceding year, and as such they were only roughly matched with probable demand. However, by the 1840s some migrant workers were taking the trouble to write to the farmers they worked for, in advance, to ascertain the state and size of the harvest. This suggests a level of education not usually associated with the more pejorative comments on the nature of the Irish agricultural workforce. In this way, Irish labour movements became far more finely tuned to the requirements of the labour market.[23]

The gypsies, unlike the Irish, were not considered respectable. They do not appear to have been integrated into the labour force, but only to have been used when other labour was not available. They were considered lawless and a threat to both people and property.[24]

In addition to the itinerant workers, some general labourers, artisans, and even small shopkeepers from the market towns would be drawn into the agricultural labour force at harvest time, along with the entire population of the villages. At harvest, the market towns of Lincolnshire 'exhibited the appearance of general mourning, [with] nearly the whole of the houses and shops being closed, and the inhabitants engaged in the corn fields.'[25]

The standard of living of the labourer
The stratification within the workforce makes it difficult to evaluate the standard of living of the labourer, since the term covered a whole range of different jobs, different rates of pay and different conditions of service. In general, the Lincolnshire labourer was better off than most. At the beginning of the century, Young, discussing wages, considered that 'Labour is probably higher than in any other county in the kingdom'. He felt that these benefits permeated much of rural society: 'It is impossible to speak too highly of the cottage system of Lincolnshire, where land, gardens, cows, and pigs are so general in the hands of the poor.'[26]

By national standards, wages and conditions were good; certainly they were much higher than in the south. Snell lists Lincolnshire agricultural wages as the highest in England in 1833 and 1837 and as fourth highest in 1850. Clearly, on this evidence, the confined men and the regularly employed day men had reasonable incomes by contemporary standards. Nevertheless, the endemic nature of poverty-induced crime, such as theft from fields, barns and nature reserves, suggests that for many of those with less reliable employment the standard of living remained decidedly low.[27]

On the question of whether living standards rose over the period, the answer varies according to the type of labourer considered. The fully employed elite of the agricultural labour force did reasonably well, but for the mass of underemployed rural labourers, their situation remained one of survival, where income fluctuated seasonally and crisis was never far away. Richardson, in a detailed analysis of the standard of living of the agricultural labourer in Lincolnshire between 1790 and 1840, concludes that 'although agricultural wages were high, they progressed only very slowly in the long run and, until the 1820s were invariably out of phase with variations in the cost of living'.[28]

In 1831, the *Weekly Register* printed a table relating to the wealth of the labouring family (see Table 4.5). The figure used – eight shillings a week was lower than that paid in Lincolnshire, but nevertheless the

Table 4.5   The condition of the labouring poor of England

	£	s	d	£	s	d
One year's wages at 8s per week	20	16	0			
Expenses						
16 sacks potatoes				4	16	0
8 sacks of potatoes for wife and three children				3	4	0
Rent				3	3	0
A pair of shoes Mending shoes					9 3	
Shoes for wife and children				0	8	0
Various articles of clothing, including mending				3	15	0
Fuel				1	0	0
Tools, candles, soaps & numerous other little things with the occasional luxury of bread and bacon and any drink but water				3	18	0
Total				20	16	0

What a living for a family! This calculation supposes constant employment, and no sickness, and a very small family.

Source: Niles Weekly Register, 31 December 1831, p. 321

table does give an impression of the chronic poverty that faced all but the elite of the agricultural labour force. Even here the situation was far from clear-cut, as living standards were more closely allied to household incomes which might be considerably expanded where opportunities for work were available for women and children. In 1834, it was considered that women might earn nine shillings a week in summer hay-making, and five shillings and six pence in the winter, turnip dragging and stone picking. At harvest it was possible to earn twelve shillings. The annual average was estimated at five shillings a week, or almost half that of the male labourer. At this level of earnings, the Caistor churchwarden felt that families could subsist (provided the price of flour did not rise too high), but they would be unable to save any money.[29]

In this instance, the stage of the family cycle has to be considered. For the day labourer, in particular, there were strong economic arguments why his family should work. In 1867, confined labourers were paid between £40 and £45 on the Wolds. Day labourers, on the other hand, were paid between 15 and 18 shillings a week, a figure which could double during the harvest period. However, in addition to this harvest supplement, the earnings of the rest of the family were important. Edward Heneage (in support of the use of child labour) stated, 'If the labour of boys under 11 years of age is prohibited, the labourer will in some cases lose half his income, as where a man has three boys 11, 10 and 9 earning respectively 10d, 8d and 6d a day.'[30]

Child labour may have been the perfect solution to the problem of limited labour supply. It was also a crucial element in the survival of the independent day labourer. Hasbach suggests that the income of a married agricultural labourer with four children over the age of 10 might be twice that of an unmarried agricultural labourer. Families with children too young to work were more likely to experience poverty than those with children of working age.[31]

The problem, of course, is distinguishing to what extent the apparent labour shortage on the Wolds actually benefited the labourer. It is difficult to know whether the shortage of labour led to increased wages, or whether the shortage was only in the eyes of the farmer who would have preferred a plentiful supply of good quality labour available at low wages. Certainly the situation in a bad winter could be dire for the day labourer. In 1861, the *Market Rasen Weekly Mail* (a paper not noted for its liberal tendencies) called for some kind of soup kitchen to be set up to help the labourers of Binbrook, in addition to the charities that had already been given out by the curate. Indeed, by the end of the 1870s, soup kitchens and charity doles contributed significantly to the welfare of an impoverished workforce at the bottom of the economic ladder in an agricultural depression. Such institutions continued to the end of the century.[32]

While the division of labour within the workplace was highly stratified, it would be a mistake to consider the labour force as static. During his working life, the agricultural labourer might move from being an unmarried junior waggoner 'living in', to being a senior hand in a tied cottage, to casual work as a day labourer. Position occupied might well vary with the age of the labourer. A male at the height of his physical powers and with a range of farming experience might occupy a secure and senior position between the ages of 30 and 45, while advancing age might reduce his economic prospects. It is quite possible that labourers moved in and out of different classes of work at various times. Where such mobility did occur, it was likely to break down any social and cultural barriers that could have developed between say, senior hands and day men, since theirs was a shared existence. The labourer had far more in common with his fellow labourers, whether of a similar grade in the hierarchy or otherwise, than he did with any other grouping. This sense of belonging to a particular group can be seen in the social world of the labourer, whether at prayer in the chapel, processing through the streets with his friendly society, or at the annual hiring fairs.[33]

The farmer and the labourer
Hiring
The hiring of a labourer by a farmer marked the beginning of an economic relationship which involved a variety of obligations. The farmer received work, the labourer received wages and possibly a variety of additional benefits such as housing and food.[34]

For much of the 19th century, agricultural servants were hired by the year at a 'statute' or hiring fair usually, but not always, held in the various market towns. Fairs were regularly held in the main towns and in larger villages such as Hainton, where during the 1860s, 1,500 attended. The nature of the fair as a human market is graphically illustrated by Hardy in *Far from the Madding Crowd*.[35]

Even at a relatively early date, the fair was far more than simply a place where laboureres were hired. The statute at Market Rasen in 1851 contained 'as usual, a variety of booths belonging to the mountebank fraternity, and minor exhibitions; the most attractive amongst which was a splendid collection of waxwork, together with a moving panorama of Palestine contained in a group of seven travelling carriages: these appear to give general satisfaction.'[36]

At Binbrook the following year, 'The town was enlivened by the Binbrook band parading the streets, Sir Montague Cholmeley being on a private visit there. There were Jefferies' and Chappell's corps of rope-dancers &c., and plenty of stalls for the sale of finery, eatables, and trash.'[37]

Servants, even after being hired, attended the next one during the week as a social event. Indeed, for many, the hiring fairs were the most important social event in their lives. 'On the appointed day, and at the appointed time and place, all the unengaged boys and girls within a radius of many miles may be seen collecting, smartly dressed in their Sunday clothes and cheerily welcoming the arrival of some recently found friend.'[38]

The week of the hiring fair provided the only opportunity for

> the yearly gathering under their father's roof of brothers and sisters from far and near, who but for this old established custom, would probably barely ever meet after they were parted, while yet children, and scattered in distant villages as farm servants.
>
> The ... week is something to look forward to – a point of interest and anticipation in their somewhat monotonous lives. The abolition of this holiday would be an undoubted loss to those whose lives of unremitting toil are too much allied already to the beasts that perish.[39]

Sidney, writing in 1848, noted: 'The custom of hiring servants at annual statute fairs still prevails in Lincolnshire. Many respectable people wish to put an end to these fairs, but the peasantry insist upon them, well knowing that there are not too many holidays in England.'[40]

During the first half of the century, the hiring fair was accepted as necessary by both hirer and hired. However, by mid-century, the hiring fair came to be considered disreputable by the 'respectable' classes. This was largely as a consequence of the 'reformation of manners' which accompanied the change in lifestyle of the farmer, and the more rigid capitalist labour relations that were now developing, with fewer labourers living-in and an increased social distance between farmer and farm worker.

Attacks on the evil of hiring fairs also came from religious quarters. The fair was a 'slavemarket, the master regards and appreciates the articles he is in quest of only in a marketable and commercial point of view'. It represented 'a deep-rooted and widespread evil that is ever undermining the morality of our agricultural servants'. Perhaps more importantly for the clergy it was a scene of 'rioting and drunkenness' to which were drawn 'the idle, the profligate, and the abandoned of the surrounding district, and for the purpose of plying their nefarious trades, thither also assemble the professional thieves and prostitutes of the neighbouring towns'.[41]

The rector of Hawerby described the Louth statute in similar terms:

The farm lads and servant girls from 12 upwards will go from one to the others [statutes]; and, if hired at the first, will often stipulate to go to the others. They have just received their year's wages, and have therefore plenty of money. It is degrading to the servant to be chosen as you would choose an ox, and the immorality that ensues is frightful. Public houses open early, and by 10 a.m. there will be dancing in all of them, and the lads halfway to drunkenness. Then the next morning will find them repeating it somewhere else .... I think them entirely vicious and unnecessary.[42]

These descriptions of base immorality provide us with glimpses of another side of the statute. Apart from religious disapproval, some farmers also wanted to see an end to this form of hiring for other reasons. In 1857, a declaration was printed in the *Stamford Mercury* which considered hiring to be 'highly detrimental to the interests of the Employers, as well as injurious to the morals of the Employed, it advocated the establishment of Offices for the purpose of Registering the Names of Heads of Families requiring Servants, as also of Servants (Male and Female) requiring Situations.'[43]

The declaration was signed by 104 people, mainly farmers, resident in north-east Lincolnshire. After a series of meetings in late 1857 and early 1858, the Lincolnshire General Servants' Amelioration Society was formed, its principal aim being the abolition of hirings and the establishment of employment offices. Similar societies were formed elsewhere at about this time. The success of the society is questionable, as there was considerable opposition to the idea not only from the employees, but also from many farmers who seemed to prefer the existing form of hiring. Newspapers, with their more urban middle-class attitudes, were hostile to the statutes and favoured the growth of employment offices, yet the *Stamford Mercury* of 15 February 1861 could only report that the Society's Annual meeting was very poorly attended, and that the employment offices had: 'experienced very indifferent success during the past year'.[44]

The growth of newspapers also resulted in employers' advertising in local papers. Thus in 1874 Cornelius Stovin 'sent an advertisement for a shepherd, and received an application ... from Charles Fletcher of Little Carlton'. Little Carlton is 13 miles away from Binbrook but would have received the same Louth-based newspapers.[45]

Unfavourable reports of the May Fair, as it came to be known, continued through the 1880s. In fact, by this time statutes had become, by and large, relict economic features, but they were still very important social occasions for the labourers. The Caistor Statute of 1877 provides a good example of how the fair had developed. There were very few servants and little hiring was done.

> The market place presented a busy appearance with roundabouts, shooting galleries, striking and lifting machines and small booths containing the 'wonders of the world' &c. Great efforts were made by the proprietors and fraternity to catch the loose pence of the pleasure seekers but we noticed very little business was done by

them. There was, we are glad to state, no drunkenness observable in the streets.[46]

However, we again need to be careful of making sweeping generalizations about the rate of decline of the fair as an economic event. Only one week after the Caistor fair, the fair in Grimsby was reportedly well attended and wages were high, while in Market Rasen more hiring was done at the May-day market than at the statute. The 1884 May hiring at Louth was described as 'a large attendance of servants and others .... 1700 persons came by rail alone and a large number arriving by other means the town presented a busy appearance during the whole of the day.' However, the same newspaper described the Alford statute as less successful.[47]

The fairs were important social events; people moved from one to the next during their one week holiday, even if they had already been hired, renewing acquaintances and enjoying the entertainments and drinking that was readily available as these fairs slowly but surely changed their function to something more approximating today's fair.[48]

Hiring fairs appear to have declined at a much earlier date in southern England. This decline is usually seen as a consequence of an increase in labour surplus which reduced ties between the farmer and the labourer. However, on the Lincolnshire Wolds, farmers still perceived a shortage of labour well into the 1870s which, combined with problems of cottage provision, meant that hiring and living-in continued to be important. There is certainly evidence of the continued importance of the fairs on the Wolds until at least the First World War. Their decreased importance as events for hiring, and the consequent shift in emphasis towards a purely social event can be considered as a consequence of the changing nature of labour relations on the farms.

Changes in the farmer's lifestyle

As the century progressed and Wold farmers became richer and more recognizably different from their workforce, their increasingly middle-class lifestyle led to considerable changes in their relationship with their labourers. Living-in, where the labourers lived in the farmhouse and may even have eaten at the same table as the farmer and his family, had been commonplace during the 18th century and the early part of the 19th century. Indeed, the ratio of workers living-in to those living in their own cottages in Lincolnshire was still high in 1851: 1:3 compared with the national extremes of 1:30 in Essex and 1:1.5 in the West Riding. According to the Lincolnshire custom, the men were fed at the farmhouse, with the single men boarding at the foreman's house. Towards the end of the century, however, the numbers of living-in labourers had fallen, and agricultural labourers more usually boarded with either the bailiff/foreman or with other agricultural labourers. There was an increased social distance between 'master' and 'men' perfectly illustrated by the actions of Cornelius Stovin who in 1872 was 'enclosing the garden for Smith (foreman) and Coney (agricultural labourer). My Lizzie (wife) will feel it a relief to have a little more privacy in her garden. It has always been distasteful to her seeing labourers' wives entering upon the seclusion.'[49]

The broadside ballad, the 'New fashioned farmer', scornfully highlighted these changes:

> In former times, both plain and neat, they'd go to church on
>   Sunday,
> Then to harrow, plough or sow they'd go upon a Monday,
> But now, instead of the plough tail, o'er hedges they are jumping,
> Instead of sowing of their corn their delight is in fox hunting,
>
> The farmers' daughters used to work all at the spinning wheel sir,
> Now such furniture as that is thought quite ungenteel sir
> Their fingers they're afraid to spoil with all such kind of sport sir,
> And sooner than a mop or broom they'd handle a pianoforte, sir.[50]

The large farmers in many ways withdrew from village society although, as we have seen, they still dominated village politics and local government. The increased social divide between tenant farmer and labourer was one which, ironically, Stovin complained about when he moved in later life to a smaller farm on the marsh at Hogsthorpe: 'I descended the hills and tracked through the flat marsh. I felt a great difference between the wold and marsh people. There is not so much distinction between classes. They run together in a kind of social blend. We hear more at Binbrook about class and mass.'[51]

This was the contrast between two distinctive pays, the Wolds with large landholdings, large farms, wealthy tenants and scientific farming, and the Lincolnshire marshes with much more fragmented landownership patterns and small holdings.

Life for the small to medium farmer was, of course, very different from that of his larger counterparts. The smaller-scale farmers had always worked in the fields along with their labourers. Often the smaller occupiers also took up profitable sidelines to help make ends meet. These men were often prepared to assist their larger neighbours, and in return might borrow horses or machinery to cultivate their own holdings.[52]

Rural protest

Charitable occasions, such as those outlined above, might suggest that interactions between farmer and labourer were largely uncontroversial and indeed socially desirable. However, there were occasions when the consensus broke down and open conflict resulted. There were also many other occasions when the consensus was maintained only shakily, where covert protest might be resorted to on the one hand and open coercion on the other.

At various times different groups within the poorer classes of society were engaged in rural protest. Food riots occurred in the first half of the century. Motives were varied, ranging from hunger and unemployment to personal grievances. At times, the covert act of arson turned into an overt celebration. On occasions, labourers took wood to help the blaze burn more, firemen were shot at, hoses cut, and helpers beaten up.[53]

The two major events of the period which resulted in the breakdown of the fragile balance were 'Captain Swing' in the early 1830s and the 'Revolt of the Field' in the 1870s. 'Captain Swing' was the name given to an outbreak of rural unrest, principally arson and machine breaking, which peaked between 1830 and 1832. The pattern of unrest varied but was found across much of England south of the Humber. In the case of Lincolnshire, relatively few threshing machines were damaged, but arson appears to have been more prevalent. 'Swing' was also the name given to a mythical stranger responsible for inciting violence among the local peasantry. The labouring classes might well add to these stories of strangers, tramps, and radicals in order to divert attention from more local culprits. The local press reinforced the national stereotypes of 'Swing':

> Many suspicious strangers have been seen in the neighbourhood, both on foot and on horseback, some of whom have been known to enquire the character of farmers, and particularly as to those that use threshing machines; unhappily none of them have yet been taken.[54]

Protest by the labourer was mainly covert and took a variety of forms such as animal maiming, arson, and threatening letters as well as rioting. At Baumber, a farmer received a letter stating, 'If you have a machine in your yard, we will set fire to the stacks the first opportunity ... you and all the farmers must give better wages to the labourers or we will fire.'[55]

It seems likely that unemployment and low wages lay at the heart of rural discontent. Disaffection during the 'Captain Swing' disturbances was most marked in towns such as Spilsby, which acted as central places not just for the Wolds, but also for the marshland, which suffered disproportionately from the depressed state of agriculture at this time. With hindsight, the churchwarden at Caistor laid the blame for the riots and incendiarism in his local area firmly on 'a threatened deduction in wages.'[56]

This certainly appears to have been the major cause, although there were others:

> The panic among the Lincolnshire farmers is universal, particularly such as have thrashing machines on their premises. Many have received threatening letters: and the breaking of machinery, and conflagration of property, form the unvarying theme of conversation amongst all ranks of society.[57]

'Captain Swing' spread steadily from southern England during the later months of 1830; by December 1830 suspected arson had been reported at Swaby on the southern Wolds where 'a wheat stack belonging to Mr Kemp ... was fired'. Further fires were reported at

Market Rasen and Horncastle. Such activity increased during 1831. Incendiarism was reported in Louth, Raithby, Ulceby near Spilsby, and Thoresway. Threatening letters were received in the Barton-on-Humber area and at Baumber.[58]

In 1832 the judge at the Assizes in Lincoln stated 'that a serious picture was presented of the extreme moral depravity of the lower orders, and of their contempt for the laws. To such a pitch had this arrived in many districts, that farmers were compelled to keep a nightly watch upon their premises.'[59]

Responses varied. Some farmers increased their wages, others removed their threshing machines, some landlords reduced rents, while some clergy reduced tithes. The more usual response, however, was to enrol special constables, form Voluntary Cavalries, or Societies for the Prosecution of Felons. At Horncastle, 'upwards of 170 householders have … enrolled as special constables … in consequence of a disposition shown by a number of labourers in the neighbourhood to create a riot, several gentlemen are embodying themselves into a regular armed association for the protection of property.'

In Caistor, sufficient 'conservators of the public peace' were sworn in that 'there is confident expectation that no incendiaries will venture to disturb the town.' Meanwhile, 'The inhabitants of Market Rasen, and the respectable farmers in its neighbourhood, are enrolling themselves to form a corps of Volunteer Cavalry (Ayscoughe Boucherett, Esq. of Willingham House, to be Captain). Already a considerable number have joined.'[60]

The Market Rasen Corps provided a military presence, with units located along the margins of the Wolds in the towns of Alford, Horncastle, Market Rasen, Caistor, and Barton. Its creation was considered necessary to counteract the perceived threat of disturbance, or worse, insurrection.[61]

Swing may have died down by the end of 1832, but arson cases continued through the 1830s, 1840s, and 1850s. Arson was clearly perceived as a major threat. At Market Rasen, the 'Association for Prosecuting Felons' resolved 'That a reward of fifty pounds be offered for the discovery of any Offender … who shall hereafter wilfully or maliciously set on fire any House … Building, Stack … the property of a member of this Association.' Rewards for prosecution could be even higher; £225 was offered at Scrivelsby in 1844.[62]

In similar vein, the Horncastle Horse Association, founded in 1836, established a mutual protection society for horse owners, going to great lengths to apprehend horse thieves.[63]

Throughout the 1830s, incidents occur which suggest that discontent was simmering below the surface. These instances also illustrate the darker side of farmer–labourer relationships. At Wold Newton, in 1832, Mr Maurice Wright the farmer, gave notice to a labourer's family. This notice was ignored. Ultimately Wright

> sent two men after the expiration of a month to render the house uninhabitable by taking off the thatch. The prisoner (the labourer's wife), in a state of excessive rage, (her husband having removed to labour elsewhere), assaulted the men by throwing stones and striking with a poker, for which she was knocked down in return. She also cut down the windows and doors, and was seen to put them on a fire made in the floor of her cottage, till the flames reached the ceiling … the place was entirely consumed.[64]

Suspicion between farmer and labourer remained in the period subsequent to Swing. In 1833 Samuel Anyan, formerly of Wyham, was found not guilty of sending a threatening letter to Mr Samuel Robson, a farmer at Wyham. Arson cases occurred at South Thoresby in 1841, Kirmond Le Mire in 1842, Binbrook in 1843, 1844 and 1852, Scrivelsby in 1844–5, Swaby and Rothwell in 1844, and at Ludford Parva in 1852. Arson and the threatening letter remained, along with poaching, the traditional resort of the poor.[65]

Punishment was usually draconian. Two teenagers found guilty of firing two straw stacks in Binbrook were sentenced to seven years transportation, while the judge in the Ludford case considered the 'crime was really so prevalent and was so dangerous … that it was rendered quite impossible that he could inflict less than the full severity of the law – fifteen years transportation each.'[66]

In 1843, the *Stamford Mercury* reported on 'Another of those agrarian outrages showing the deep-seated discontent of the labouring classes

passing through the village of Cabourne he met, and stood talking with, a fellow unionist, Edwards. Charles Henry Brown, a farmer from Cook's own village of Swallow, rode up, probably also on his way home from the weekly market. He joined in the conversation, and soon high words were flying. Farmer Brown said he would ride over a laneful of men such as Edwards and Cook, who backed away a pace at a time, until he was driven against a hedge. To protect himself he then struck Brown's stick out of his hand, and fended off the horse by striking it over the head. If Brown was surprised at this display of spirit, he had more in store for him, for Cook, doubtless aided by his union, proceeded to have him charged with assault. The magistrates' bench of five squires and parsons were obviously embarrassed by the case, which they must have known was being followed with widespread interest .... Brown's lawyer made offers to Cook, and the magistrates suggested that the matter be settled without their help, but Cook pressed for them to dispose of the case. Finally Brown was convicted and fined one shilling plus costs. The case was reported and commented upon by an anonymous correspondent of the Labour League Examiner. He suggested that if John Cook, unionist and labourer, had tried to ride down Charles Henry Brown, he would have received three months' imprisonment with hard labour.[104]

The close geographical proximity of judge and defendant can only have added to social conflict and fuelled any feelings of social injustice. For instance, the rector of Binbrook, J. T. Huntley, sat in the police court in his own parish. His lack of sympathy with the plight of the poor was clearly shown in November 1865, when he sentenced William Bond to one month's hard labour for soliciting alms. Actions of this kind almost certainly reinforced local perceptions of the Church as a pillar of the ruling class. Indeed, the politics of the clergy were largely Conservative, a reflection of their economic interests, a further factor alienating them from rural nonconformists.[105]

The agricultural labour force was highly stratified. There was a world of difference between the life of, say, the farm bailiff on a large Wold farm, and an itinerant Irish labourer moving from farm to farm during the harvest season. It would thus be a mistake to accept any simplistic notions of the agricultural labourer, whether of the self-deprecating 'Hodge' variety, or the more class-based, 'agricultural-labourer-as-proletarian' variety.

Thus we have to consider the agricultural labourer in two ways; first and foremost as an employee working the land, and second, as a member of a distinct, but not necessarily homogenous or even harmonious, grouping within rural society. We must take care not to oversimplify so as to produce a stereotyped 19th-century rural labourer, or worse, a caricatured 19th-century rural labourer.

Tensions were at their greatest at times of economic depression. Profitable agriculture did not necessarily mean that the casual labourer would share the benefits with the farmer, but unprofitable agriculture certainly guaranteed that the labourer would suffer first. 'The labourer was not short of lords and masters. The parson and his wife at the rectory, the squire, and his tenants, the farmers, who in their turn exercised considerable control over the daily lives of the agricultural labourer and his family.'[106]

In many ways, it is difficult to evaluate the role of the labourer within society, since he has left relatively few written accounts, and contemporary records usually considered him merely in the context of the farm or domestic servant. The only comprehensive coverage of the labourer occurs at times of overt social conflict when the labourer is seen to be acting illegally or seditiously. This enables us to paint a picture of certain major episodes, but does not provide much insight into the more humdrum existence of the labourer.

Nevertheless, it is clear that the role of the labourer on the Lincolnshire Wolds shifted significantly during the century. The labourer at the beginning of the century was much closer to the farmer – socially and economically. As agriculture was transformed, living-in in the farmhouse declined, and new forms of relationships developed between farmer and labourer, partly as a result of changing agricultural techniques and partly due to changing social conditions. This in turn led to issues such as adequate provision of cottages becoming increasingly important, and in many cases forced labourers to walk greater distances to work from the inadequate housing they could barely afford which was available mainly in the larger villages. Undoubtedly social distancing and spatial segregation occurred as a result of changes in employment practices.

By the final quarter of the century, many of the younger and more able-bodied men were leaving the land, either to work in the towns or for new lives in the colonies. The labourers that remained lived in a very different rural society from that of their forebears a century before.

Notes to Chapter 4

1   For an overview see J. Beckett, 'English rural society, 1750–1914', *The Historian,* 38 (1993), pp. 10–12.
2   C. Kightly, *Country oices,* London, 1984, p. 46.
3   1851 CEB. *Journals of a Methodist farmer 1871–1875,* ed. J. Stovin, London, 1982, p. 124. BPP. 1867. *First report of the Commissioners on the employment of children, young persons and women in agriculture,* Appendix Part 1. Mr Stanhope's report, p. 278.
4   A. Young, *General view of the agriculture of the county of Lincoln,* Newton Abbott, 1813, pp. 462, 466–7.
5   BPP. *Report of the select committee on agricultural distress, 1836,* paras 5853–73. BPP, *Report of the special assistant poor law commissioners on the employment of women and children in agriculture, 1843.* Evidence of Mr Booth of Kelstern, p. 254.
6   BPP. *Report of the Poor Law Commissioners, 1834.*
7   P. Pusey, 'On the agricultural improvements of Lincolnshire', *Journal of the Royal Agricultural Society of England,* 4 (1843), p. 315.
8   BPP. *Children in agriculture, 1867,* pp. 282, 284.
9   BPP. *Women and children in agriculture, 1843,* p. 255. S. Sidney, *Railways and agriculture in North Lincolnshire,* Pickering, 1848, p. 48.
10 BPP. *Children in agriculture, 1867.*
11 ibid.
12 BPP. *Women and children in agriculture, 1867,* p. 286.
13 BPP. *Women and children in agriculture, 1843,* p. 1.
14 BPP. *Children in agriculture, 1867,* p. 253.
15 ibid.
16 BPP. *Children's employment commission.* Report of Mr F. D. Lange, 1867, pp. 15–16. See, for instance, the evidence of the Rev. W. Smythe of Elkington Hall and Mr Edward Locock of Elkington Grange, p. 13. BPP. *Women and children in agriculture, 1867,* p. 283, evidence of J. J. Mackintosh.
17 Sidney, *Railways,* 1848, p. 89.

18   It is impossible to assess accurately the full extent of the gangs. Neale,
     for instance, is listed in the Census enumerators books only as an
     agricultural labourer. BPP. *Women and children in agriculture, 1867*, p. 278.
19   LAO. Misc Dep 221. The Dairies of Fanny Fieldsend. 3 August 1884.
     LRSM, 16 August 1861. E. J. T. Collins, 'The rationality of surplus
     agricultural labour: mechanisation in English agriculture in the 19th
     century', *AHR*, 35 (1987), p. 49; S. Barber, 'Irish migrant agricultural
     labourers in 19th century Lincolnshire', *Saothar.*, 8 (1982), pp. 10–11.
     E. J. T. Collins, 'Migrant labour in British agriculture in the 19th
     century,' *Economic History Review*, 29 (1976), p. 52. J. H. Johnson,
     'Harvest migration from 19th century Ireland', *Transactions of the
     Institute of British Geographers*, 41 (1967), p. 99. Johnson concentrates
     mainly on the place of origin of these labourers in Ireland. For a more
     general picture see A. Redford, *Labour migration in England, 1800–1850,*
     Manchester, 1976 and J. Saville, *Rural depopulation in England and Wales*,
     1851–1951, London, 1957.
20   PRO. MH12 6738, 22 February 1837.
21   *LNLA*, 11 December 1880. J. A. Perkins, 'Harvest technology and
     labour supply in Lincolnshire and the East Riding of Yorkshire,
     1750–1850', *Labour and Tillage,* 3 (1976), pp. 51–3, 56. *LNLA*, 7
     December 1861.
22   Collins, 'Migrant labour', p. 51.
23   Perkins, 'Harvest technology', pp. 52–3. Barber, 'Irish migrant
     labourers', p. 21.
24   *LNLA*, 16 November 1861. *LRSM*, 7 June 1844.
25   Cited in Perkins, 'Harvest technology', p. 52.
26   Young, *General view*, pp. 451, 468–9.
27   K. D. M. Snell, *Annals of the labouring poor: social change and agrarian
     England 1660–1900*, Cambridge, 1985, p. 130. T. L. Richardson, 'The
     agricultural labourers' standard of living in Lincolnshire, 1790–1840:
     social protest and public order', *AHR*, 41 (1993), p. 3.
28   For a discussion see J. Rule, *The labouring classes in early industrial
     England, 1750–1850*, London, 1986, ch. 1. Richardson, 'Standard of
     living'.
29   BPP. *Poor law commissioners, 1834.*
30   BPP. *Children in agriculture, 1867*, p. 280.
31   W. Hasbach, *A history of the English agricultural labourer,* London, 1920, p.
     226.
32   *MRWM*, 19 January 1861. *LNLA*, 30 January 1886, 7 March 1888.
33   See for instance R. Jefferies, *Hodge and his masters*, London, 1966 for a
     view of country life in the 1860s and 1870s, and Snell, *Annals*.

5

SOCIETY ON THE LINCOLNSHIRE WOLDS

The previous three chapters have considered the roles of the landowner, the tenant farmer, and the labourer within society. As we have seen, the ownership of land provided the landlord with significant economic, social, and political influence. Their interactions with their tenantry and the workforce either directly as employer of labour or indirectly through their tenants had far reaching consequences for society as a whole. Variations in landownership patterns resulted, in part, in differences between communities. The ways in which these differences developed and the subsequent effect these differences had on social interactions were of critical importance to the way the Lincolnshire Wolds evolved during the 19th century.

This chapter attempts to show how a distinctive sense of place developed, as a consequence of market forces, patterns of landownership, political legislation, social movements, and the physical geography of the area. The first part of the chapter looks at variations in landownership patterns. This is followed by a discussion of variations in the types of occupation found on the Wolds. Subsequently, differences in household structures and the provision of cottage accommodation are considered along with a range of demographic characteristics. Finally, the chapter looks at how these differences had an impact on the broader social life of the Wolds. It will become clear that there were significant links between patterns of landownership, the nature of farming, the composition of the agricultural workforce, and the provision of trades and services. As a result, the larger villages evolved with social structures that were quite distinct from those in the smaller villages.[1]

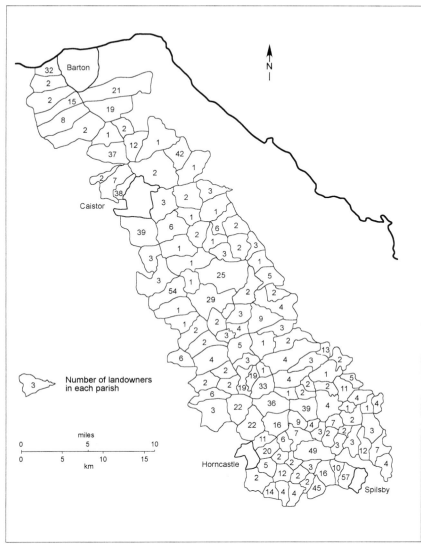

Fig. 40   Landownership on the Lincolnshire Wolds, 1831
Source: LAO. 1831 Land Tax Assessments

Variations in landownership

Figure 40 shows the number of landowners in each parish at the beginning of the 1830s, using the land tax assessments. As we have

**Fig. 41 Landownership on the central and
northern Wolds, 1831**

already seen, landownership on the Wolds was highly concentrated.
Eighty-six of the parishes were in the hands of six or fewer landowners.
This pattern was in marked contrast to the more fragmented nature of

landownership on both the Fens and the coastal marshes. Indeed, of the 78 parishes to the south of Grimsby, which comprised the inner and outer marsh, 49 had more than 20 landowners and only 11 had six or fewer landowners. A similar pattern of fragmented landownership continues on the Fens to the south of the Wolds.[2]

In those parishes where most of the land was owned by one landlord, that fact might have a significant influence on the way in which society developed in that parish. This was particularly likely to be the case where these large landowners were resident in the parish (see Chapter 2). However, there are dangers in oversimplifying the role of the landowner. A more detailed study of parishes on the central and northern Wolds (see Figure 41) provides specific examples to illustrate this point. There were seven parishes where landownership was concentrated in the hands of a resident landowner: Brocklesby, the home of Lord Yarborough; North Willingham, the residence of the Boucheretts; South Elkington, home of the Smyths; Swinhope, the residence of the Alingtons; Hawerby, owned by Theophilius Harneis; Cuxwold, owned by the Thorolds; and Riby, owned by George Tomline. At first glance these parishes might appear similar. However, a closer inspection of the seven parishes shows marked differences. Yarborough, Alington, Smyth, Boucherett, and Harneis were primarily resident in their parishes. Tomline had other houses which were at least equally important as family residences, while the Thorolds were not always resident at Cuxwold. Brocklesby was Yarborough's principal residence although he did have properties elsewhere. These different levels of involvement at the local scale would have affected the local community in a range of ways. Similarly, social differences between these landowners had an impact. While Yarborough and Tomline can be considered as landed magnates, Boucherett and Smyth both belonged to the middling ranks of the gentry, while Alington (1,200 acres), Thorold (1,543 acres), and Harneis (450 acres) had relatively small estates. Thus the influence of these men was bound to vary, due both to their place of residence and their relative wealth and social position. To illustrate this point, we have already seen how the Yarboroughs created a typical Victorian estate village at Brocklesby; in

Agricultural work was the principal employment in all parishes on the Wolds, except Brocklesby, Somersby, and Harrington, where large gentry households resulted in greater numbers of domestic servants. However, as might be expected, there were considerable differences between parishes. The larger parishes had lower percentages of agricultural workers than the average, as did those parishes with resident landowners. Other small parishes had high percentages employed in agriculture, reflecting the dominance of agricultural work in these parishes. This contrasts with the more diverse employment base of the larger villages and the greater importance of domestic service in those parishes with resident landowners (see Table 5.1).[8]

Table 5.1   The occupation structure of the labour force on the Lincolnshire Wolds, 1851

Village population	Agriculture		Domestic service		Trades and crafts	
	no.	%	no	%	no.	%
Larger than 400	2,721	56	989	20	1,169	24
0–400	4,727	64	1,786	24	894	12
Parish with resident landowner	1,231	57	665	31	258	12

Source: Census Enumerators Books

Service employment

Alongside work in agriculture, a second major occupational category open to the labouring classes was domestic service. This work was mainly undertaken by females. Generally, numbers employed in domestic service reached unprecedented heights during the Victorian period. Every self-respecting middle-class household was expected to have a number of servants, and the number employed reflected social station. The whole system was sufficiently formalized that Mrs Beeton could publish precise guidelines as to how many servants a household should have, and what the various grades of servant should be paid.[9]

Parishes with a resident landowner had the highest percentage of domestic servants in their workforce. In 1851, 58 percent of the labour force in Brocklesby was in service, reflecting the importance of the earl of Yarborough's household. Apart from the landowners, the second group which employed large numbers of servants were the larger farmers. An analysis of farm households in the 1851 Census indicates this clearly. In a sample of 32 parishes on the north and central Wolds, there were only 12 domestic servants resident on the 60 farms of less than 100 acres (0.2 servants/farm), while the 126 farms of more than 100 acres had 285 domestic servants resident (2.3 servants/farm) (see Figure 43a). The larger farms (over 500 acres) had an even larger number of domestic servants living-in (59 farms with 186 domestic servants – 3.2 servants/farm) (see Figure 43b). These findings can be equated with the social position of the wealthier farmers who effectively can be considered as gentlemen farmers occupying a similar role to the local gentry in other areas of the country (see Chapter 3). The more substantial elements of the clergy, the tithe-receiving rectors and the so-called 'squarsons', were also major employers of domestic servants.

A word of caution is needed here concerning the occupational classifications used in the 19th-century census returns. The term 'servants in husbandry' was commonly used for farm workers who lived-in on the farm, while domestic servants might be termed as 'in service'. At times, due to inconsistencies between enumerators, it is almost impossible to distinguish between these categories. In addition, Higgs has argued that there are four possible areas where significant under-recording of occupations may have taken place. First, there was probably an underestimation of seasonal labour (the census usually took place in March/April); second, some workers were excluded who were not given occupational titles; third, the female relations of farmers were often not given employment descriptions; and finally, some rural workers placed in categories other than agriculture were not recorded.[10]

Bearing in mind these caveats, the parishes with the smallest proportions of domestic servants fall into two main groups: parishes where the landlord was not resident in the county and parishes with larger populations. The concentration of master–servant relationships within those smaller parishes where there were resident landowners or

**Fig. 43 Number of servants resident on farms on the
north and central wolds, 1851**

(a) Over 110 acres

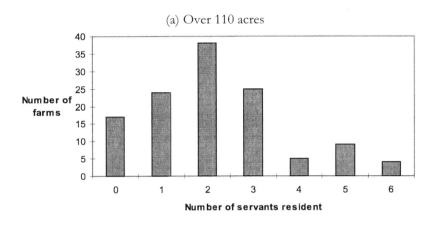

(b) Over 500 acres

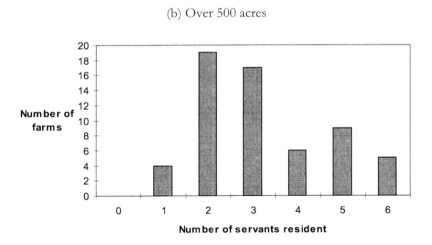

large-scale tenant farmers and the relative absence of such relationships
from the larger villages increased the social differences between the
village types.

Employment in trades and crafts

As we might anticipate, the larger the population of a Wolds village, the greater the percentage of the working population involved in trades and services (see above, Table 5.1), and the wider range of services available.

Table 5.2   Employment in trades and crafts in selected Wold villages, 1851

Occupation	Large villages			Small villages		
	Binbrook	Ludford	Tealby	Kelstern	Walesby	Thorganby
Baker	33	1	2	-	-	-
Blacksmith	15	4	6	5	2	2
Bricklayer/ builder	9	6	14	-	-	-
Brickmaker	1	-	1	-	-	-
Butcher	5	1	2	-	-	-
Shoemaker	16	7	8	-	-	-
Draper	7	3	6	-	-	-
Grocer	6	3	4	-	-	-
Miller	7	4	3	-	2	-
Plumber	3	-	3	-	1	-
Publican	2	1	2	-	-	-
Saddler	2	-	1	-	-	-
Tailor/ dressmaker	33	6	13	1	2	2
Wheelwright	15	3	6	1	3	3
Carrier	4	4	2	-	1	-
Druggist	2	-	2	-	-	-
Carpenter	11	5	5	1	1	-

It would be a mistake to attribute this lack of building solely to the poor laws, since it is clear that, in some instances, landlords were also unwilling to invest in buildings for the farmer – who was unlikely to become a burden on the poor rate! At Binbrook Hall, Stovin urgently requested a new farmhouse: 'The house is damp and unhealthy. It has harboured sickness now for half a century. No doubt my mother and eldest sister's days were shortened after many years of suffering. My wife has experienced an inquisitorial torture through most of the period of our married life.'[25]

Poor health was not his only concern: 'It is a great matter to have a house where respectable servants will like to live, and good stabling that a groom would take some pride in keeping in order.' Stovin finally managed to get his farmhouse rebuilt, but although two new cottages were promised as well, they were not built until 1891. In this instance, the attitude of the Denisons, Stovin's landlords, who were resident near St Albans, can be contrasted with that of the Yarboroughs, the Heneages, and the Turnors.[26]

It appears that, to some extent, the problems of housing provision were addressed during the later decades of the century. Census evidence suggests a significant growth in the number of households over the period 1851–1881 in the small parishes, which would indicate building activity in these parishes. For a sample of 27 small parishes, the number of households increased by 126 (+14%) between 1851 and 1881. The five large parishes in the same area, on the other hand, experienced a loss of 12 households (-0.01%). This evidence is strengthened when placed in the context of an overall decline in the rural population and a steady increase in the number of empty properties found in the county. Over the same period, the population of the sample area fell by 7 percent, yet the population of the smaller parishes fell by only 0.02 percent.

This growth in the provision of housing can be related to the need to retain a labour force on the farms. Several factors made this an increasingly essential requirement. Large-scale migration was taking place, both to industrial and urban areas elsewhere in England and overseas, and many of the younger and most able workers were being drawn away from the land. It became necessary therefore for farmers to be able to retain skilled labourers. The Revolt of the Field focused ideas very much on working and living conditions in agriculture, and although the unionization of the workforce was ultimately unsuccessful, there was nevertheless an increased awareness by farmers of the need to provide for their core workforce.

By the end of the century, the housing situation had all but resolved itself, largely as a result of the flight from the land. Haggard complained, 'a cottage of mine with a good garden has been standing vacant for a year because I cannot find a labouring tenant'.[27]

Population

Nationally, rural populations grew during the first half of the 19th century before declining towards the end of the century, and the Lincolnshire Wolds were no exception. Overall, populations grew until 1851 before falling. However, the southern and central areas of the Wolds continued to grow until 1861, while the northern Wolds, after a dip in numbers at the time of the 1861 census, continued to grow until 1881. In the case of Barnetby, Barton, and South Ferriby growth persisted into the present century. To a large extent, this later growth can be explained by industrial, railway, and river trade developments at a time when numbers in purely agricultural communities were declining.

Figure 47 shows the population changes for the large and small parishes. There are clear differences in rates of growth between these

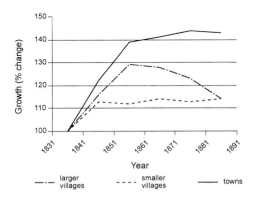

Fig. 47 Population change, 1831–1881

groups of parishes. To highlight the differences in rates of growth, 'large', 'small', and 'town' population figures have been plotted from a base of 100 in 1831. In the case of the 'large' parishes growth from a total population of 13,038 in 1831 peaked at 16,870 in 1851 before declining to 14,874 in 1881. By contrast, the small parishes grew more steadily, from 10,096 in 1831 to 11,316 in 1851, but continued to increase in population until as late as 1881 before declining during the final two decades of the century. Thus, in the inter-censal periods 1861–71 and 1871–81, the smaller parishes grew slightly, while the large parishes declined. Indeed, by 1901, of the 27 parishes with populations greater than 400 in 1851, only 14 still had populations of over 400. It appears that the smaller villages were able to retain population as they continued to house their essential core agricultural workforce, while the casual labour force of the larger villages left the land and the large central village began to lose its place in the trading hierarchy to the neighbouring towns as a result of steadily improving transport links.

If we compare the population structure of the larger and smaller villages (see Figure 48), there are several striking differences. First, the small village pyramid shows a disproportionate number of males between the ages of 10–24, 2,719 males (33% of the total male population) compared to 2,241 males (28%) in the larger villages. Unfortunately the occupational descriptions contained within the census returns do not provide sufficient detail to distinguish between servants in husbandry and agricultural labourers. Nevertheless, it was this age range which was most in demand on the large farms that dominated society in the smaller villages. Being mostly unmarried, this section of the community lived on the farm, usually with the bailiff, and were hired for the year. A second obvious difference can be seen at the base of the pyramid. There were more children under 10 resident in the larger villages than in the smaller villages as a proportion of the total population – 4,404 (28%) compared to 4,052 (25%). This pattern again reflects the workings of the housing and labour market.[28]

There was limited suitable accommodation for a labourer and his family in the smaller villages. The tendency was to provide for younger, able-bodied workers, who were usually boarded with the foreman or other senior hands.

The third major difference in age structure between the two types of parish reflected both the workings of the poor laws and the restricted supply of accommodation in the small, agricultural villages, where all available housing was required for the core of the farm workforce. The larger villages had a greater percentage of their population over the age of 60 – 1,170 people (7.5%) compared to 1,095 people (6.9%). The reasons for this difference were given by the undertaker to the Louth Union:

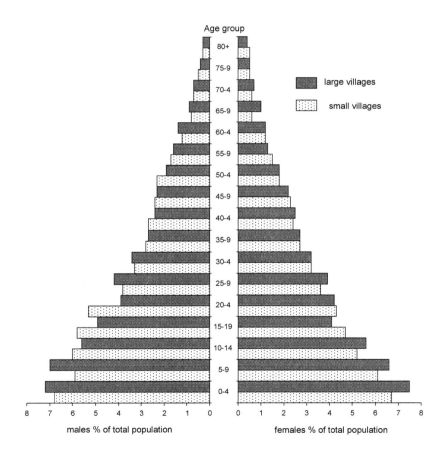

Fig. 48   Population structure, 1851

I have been employed for 14 years by the Guardians of the Louth Union to supply coffins and attend to the internment [*sic*] of all the paupers who died in the parish during that time – between 1,000 and 2,000. More than half of that number have been from different parishes composing the Union, and have been brought to Louth and died there. Of the old couples that have been compelled to break up their homes and submit to the stringent rules of the house, such as parting man and wife, several of them have not lived more than six months, and many of them not so long …. Another large proportion of the poor from the different parishes are not really compelled to go into the house, but have outdoor relief given to them; they however must come to Louth, because house room cannot be had in the village. At the present time there is an old couple living near to me … brought from a village about six miles from Louth and they have lived in the said parish for the greater part of their lives; but his house must be had for a younger man.[29]

The specific labour requirements of the smaller parishes and the economics of farming were very significant as causal factors in determining the population structure of these parishes. These requirements were then reflected, indirectly, in the population structure of the larger parishes and surrounding market towns.

Apart from the age structure of the population, a further noticeable difference between large and small parishes concerns the sex structure of the population. There were more females resident in the larger parishes than in the smaller parishes. As an overall ratio, there were 91 females for every 100 males in the small parishes, compared with 97:100 in the large parishes. Again, this reflects the demands of the labour market. Employment in the smaller parishes was dominated by males; there were only limited employment opportunities for females. The vast majority of the work available was in agriculture and was considered to be men's work. In the smaller parishes, work was restricted effectively to domestic service only (84% of all female employment), while in the larger parishes there were more opportunities for work in trades such as dressmaking (13%).

Along with the workings of the labour market, the operation of the poor laws was also instrumental in creating this sexual division of the population. Generally speaking, females were the most economically vulnerable members of the community, and therefore the most likely to end up in the workhouse. This was certainly the case in the Caistor Union workhouse where, in 1851, 58 percent of inmates were female (see Figure 49), at a time when only 49 percent of the total population in the parishes of the Union was female. While the workhouses were generally occupied more by the elderly and the very young than by the able bodied, it was the able-bodied who attracted most attention

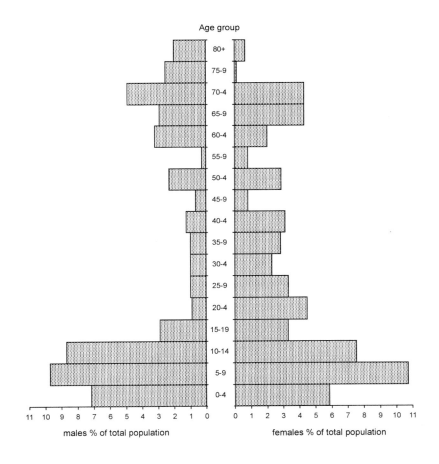

Fig. 49   The population structure of the Caistor Union Workhouse 1841–1861

relating to the cost of pauperism. It is within this category – namely between the ages of 15–65 that women seemed far more at risk than men. Indeed, there is a marked absence of males in the 15–44 age range, precisely the range when men were at the height of their earning power. In Caistor workhouse, paupers between these ages made up 38.5 percent of the population, but of these almost three-quarters (74.2 percent) were female. The possibility of bastard children and the scarcity of female work combined to make the female resident an unattractive proposition to the cost-conscious landowner or farmer.[30]

By 1881, the gender structure of the population had become more balanced. This change reflected both the increased participation of females in the labour market and the overall decline in the male population. This decline was largely a consequence of reduced demand for male labour, particularly in agriculture, where a combination of mechanization and a move away from labour-intensive arable production to grazing, following the onset of agricultural depression in the mid 1870s, led to workers leaving the land in search of employment in the towns or overseas.[31]

This discussion of a range of socio-economic variables has shown how distinct yet interconnected communities developed on the Wolds during the 19th century. In general terms, we can characterize the Wold landscapes at this time as one of small semi-isolated villages which serviced large, technologically advanced farms. These villages were usually no more than five or six miles from a centrally located larger village which provided a range of trades and services to the farms as well as housing a large proportion of the day labourers and the casual agricultural workforce.

Notes to Chapter 5

1   For a more detailed discussion of this theoretical approach see C. K. Rawding, 'Society and place in nineteenth century North Lincolnshire', *Rural History,* 3 (1992), pp. 59–67.

2   For a more detailed discussion see *Land and property: the English Land Tax, 1692–1832,* eds. M. Turner and D. Mills Gloucester, 1986. B. A. Holderness, 'Open and close parishes in England in the eighteenth and 19th centuries', *AHR,* 20 (1972), pp. 129–39, suggests that

nationally the average number of 'close' townships was about 20% rising to 40% in some areas. For practical purposes, 'close' has been defined as five or less owners of land, while a parish has been considered 'open' with 15 or more owners of land.

3   Apart from Riby Hall, Tomline also owned 1 Carlton House Terrace in London and Orwell Park, Ipswich, *Who's who of British Members of Parliament, Volume 1 1832–1885,* ed. M. Stenton, Hassocks, 1976. In addition to 8,439 acres in Lincolnshire, Tomline also had 18,473 acres in Suffolk, J. Bateman, *The acre-ocracy of England.* London, 1876. The Thorolds illustrate well the dangers of a static classification such as the one used here. The extent to which the family were resident is unclear. They built Cuxwold Hall in 1861 and certainly lived there for some time, but in the 1870s their tenant farmer, John Sowerby, was resident, and indeed bought the whole parish from them in 1877. I am grateful to the late Mr Michael Sleight for this information. Yarborough also owned Manby Hall, Brigg and 17 Arlington Street, London, M. Walford, *The county families of the United Kingdom,* London, 1877. For a brief background to the Alington family see P. Smith, *The story of Claribel (Charlotte Alington Barnard),* Lincoln, 1965, ch. 1.

4   LAO. Lindsey Quarter Sessions, 1831 Land Tax Assessments.

5   For an overview of the use of the census in the analysis of occupations see *Local communities in the Victorian Census Enumerators Books,* eds. D. R. Mills and K. Schurer, Oxford, 1996, Part II.

6   Farm size does not necessarily correlate with acreage occupied by a single farmer. Many of the wealthier tenant farmers seem to have held several farms at a time. *LRSM,* 13 March 1874. J. V. Beckett, 'The decline of the small landowner in England and Wales', in *Landowners, capitalists and entrepreneurs,* ed. F. M. L. Thompson, Oxford, 1994, pp. 104–5. D. Grigg, 'Farm size in England and Wales, from early Victorian times to the present', *AHR,* 11 (1987), p. 185. A. Howkins, 'Peasants, servants and labourers: the marginal workforce in British agriculture c.1870–1914', *AHR,* 42 (1994). p. 53.

7   See M. Reed, 'The peasantry of 19th century England, a neglected class?' *History Workshop,* 18 (1984), pp. 53–74; M. Reed, 'Nineteenth century rural England: a case for peasant studies?' *Journal of Peasant Studies,* 14 (1986), pp. 78–98. There seems to be no hard-and-fast definition of a cottager, however; in Lincolnshire at least it is never used for holdings of more than about 10 acres. D. R. Mills, *Lord and peasant in nineteenth century Britain,* London, 1980, p. 29. For the national pattern concerning farmers employing labour see M. Overton,

'Agriculture', in *Atlas of industrialising Britain: 1780–1914*, eds. J. Langton and R. J. Morris, London, 1986, pp. 43–5.

8   See C. K. Rawding, 'Village type and employment structure: an analysis in the nineteenth century Lincolnshire Wolds', *Local Population Studies*, 53 (1994), pp. 53–69.

9   P. Horn, *The rise and fall of the Victorian servant*, Gloucester, 1986. See *Culture and society in Britain, 1850–1900*, ed. J. M. Golby, Oxford, 1986, pp. 190–1.

10   E. Higgs, 'Occupational censuses and the agricultural workforce in Victorian England and Wales', *Economic History Review*, 48 (1995), pp. 700–16.

11   I am grateful to Mr Alec Thompson for allowing me unrestricted access to his family records. For a more detailed discussion see *Keelby parish and people. Part two 1831–1881*, ed. C. K. Rawding, Keelby, 1987, pp. 28–37.

12   A. Mitson and B. Cox, 'Victorian estate housing on the Yarborough estate, Lincolnshire', *Rural History*, 6 (1995), p. 33.

13   PRO. IR58 33575–7 Sched Nos. 60a, 128–38, 164, 270–81, cited in C. Rawding and B. Short, 'Binbrook in 1910: the use of the Finance (1909–1910) Act Records', *L.H.A.*, 28 (1993), pp. 58–65.

14   BPP. *First report of the commissioners on the employment of children, young persons and women in agriculture*, Appendix 1, Mr Stanhope's report, 1867.

15   BPP. *Reports from the select committee on settlement and poor removal*, 1847.

16   *LNLA*, 23 March 1861.

17   BPP. *Children in agriculture*. In the case of Heneage, Edward James Willson was employed as estate architect 1833–54 during which time George Fieschi Heneage undertook an ambitious building programme costing £76,800.

18   H. A. Clemenson, *English country houses and landed estates*, London,1982, p. 87; LAO. YARB 5/14/16. BPP. *Children in agriculture*, p. 283. LAO. YARB 9/19/2, 8 March 1847, cited in A. Mitson and B. Cox, *Victorian housing*, p. 32.

19   C. Wilson, 'Christopher Turnor: an agricultural improver', paper presented to the East Midlands industrial Archaeology conference, 24 October 1987. For a general view of model farm buildings see J. M. Robinson, *Georgian model farms: a study of decorative and model farm buildings in the age of improvement. 1700–1846*. Oxford, 1983. For a similar situation in South Lincolnshire see P. S. Barnwell, 'An extra dimension? Lincolnshire farm buildings as historical evidence', *AHR*, 46 (1998), pp. 35–46.

20   *LRSM*, 3 April 1874, quoted in R. C. Russell, *The revolt of the field in Lincolnshire*, Lincoln, 1956, p. 57.

21   *Journals of a Methodist farmer, 1871–1875*, ed. J. Stovin, London, 1982, p. 141. Caird, *English agriculture in 1850–1851*, London, 1968, p. 197.

22   BPP. *Children in agriculture,* p. 279.

23   ibid., p. 278.

24   ibid., pp. 279, 283.

25   Stovin, *Journals*, p. 141.

26   ibid.; *LNLA*, 28 January 1860.

27   H. Rider Haggard, *A farmer's year*, London, 1987, p. 408.

28   In many ways the division into five-year bands is unsatisfactory, since children generally began casual work somewhere between the ages of 6 and 10, and full-time work between the ages of 10 and 15.

29   *LNLA*, 20 October 1866.

30   See C. K. Rawding, *Poor relief and the rural workforce: a case study of north Lincolnshire, 1834–1861*, University of Sussex research paper in Geography, 16, 1986. C. K. Rawding, 'The poor law amendment act 1834–65: a case study of Caistor poor law union', *LHA*, 22 (1987), pp. 15–23; R. Pashley, *Pauperism and poor laws*, London, 1852; J. A. Perkins, 'Unmarried mothers and the poor law in Lincolnshire, 1800–1850', *LHA,* 20 (1985), pp. 21–33.

31   See R. Arnold, *The farthest promised land,* Wellington, 1981.

6

CULTURE AND CHANGE IN THE VILLAGES

We have seen that the 19th century brought significant social change to the Lincolnshire Wolds. Agriculture was transformed, towns grew during the first half of the century before stagnation set in, while the railways opened up new vistas for many and provided goods and services that previously had been extremely difficult, if not impossible to obtain. It is hardly surprising in this context that social life at the end of the century was very different indeed from that at the beginning of the century.

At the beginning of the 19th century, working hours were unregulated and pastimes focussed on a range of activities which would seem almost barbaric to later generations, including cock fighting and bear baiting, rough music and wife sales, harvest home and Plough Monday, each and every one of them liberally laced with large quantities of alcohol. This was a culture which would slowly disappear during the 19th century as the growth of Methodism, Teetotalism, the rise of the Friendly Society, and the supremacy of Victorian values brought sobriety and rational order to life on the Wolds. This was nothing less than a cultural transformation, and it is the subject of this chapter.[1]

Traditional culture was based on the customs that developed out of the rhythm of everyday life. Many of these were sustained by popular support but became increasingly at odds with the wishes of the wealthier classes in society. It was usual for the farm labourers to eat with the farmer during the 18th and early 19th centuries (see Chapter 4). The 'harvest home' was the traditional celebration of the whole community at the end of the harvest. 'Religious' activity at the beginning of the century was often merged into village life and ritual. Confirmation, for instance, was a secular celebration. After confirmation in Alford in 1837, many people went to the public houses to dance and associate with 'lewd women', while similar activities in Louth in 1840 led to 'riotous, bacchanalian and pugilistic proceedings'. Confirmation was, in many ways, viewed as being the end of childhood. As late as 1864, nearly one-third of parishes in the diocese of Lincoln celebrated communion no more than four times a year. All these practices were in marked contrast to what had become popular culture by the end of the century.[2]

By the later years of the century, many of the elements of popular culture had been either moved to the fringe of society or been replaced by alternatives, as with the arrival of the harvest festival in lieu of the harvest home. Alternatively, they may have been declared illegal as with wife sales.

To illustrate the extent of these changes, two items from the same newspaper can be cited. The *Lincolnshire Rutland and Stamford Mercury* contained the following front-page advertisement for two consecutive weeks in January 1800: 'COCK FIGHTING – New Cock-Pit Newark for 5 guineas a battle between the Gentlemen of Lincolnshire and the Gentlemen of Nottinghamshire. (on Tuesday & Wednesday 27th/28th).'[3]

Forty years later, the activity had clearly been marginalized since the tone of the same paper was rather different: 'COCK-FIGHTING We regret to learn that notwithstanding the progress of knowledge and refinement ... this barbarous and inhumane practice still obtains support in this county.'[4]

This change in tone permeated the entire paper which, during the 1840s, was remarkable for the large number of accounts it carried relating to the Temperance movement, religious activities generally, and 'respectable' social events such as village fetes

Rough music, ran-tanning or 'riding the stang' as it was known in parts of the county, was also a common feature of life in the villages. Such practices involved large numbers of people, often the young men of the village, expressing their disapproval of the activities of one person or family, by generating 'rough music' as a way of exerting what must have been significant peer pressure on the miscreants. At Binbrook, in 1841, the *Stamford Mercury* reported the return of a

stereotypical 'Victorian' values of sobriety and godliness. Social control was much more readily achieved with such festivities. This was in contrast to previous more secular celebrations usually associated with drunkenness and 'lewd' behaviour. [20]

Changes in agrarian capitalism led to significant changes in life-style and culture. In many ways, this phase marked the transition from the moral economy of the pre-industrial period to a more fully-fledged set of capitalist social relations in the later period. The progressive marginalization of the hiring fair as a means of employing labour has already been discussed. Traditional patterns of recreation were regarded as 'wasteful of time and money, as threats to property and public order, and as remnants of a primitive past. Popular recreations were seen to be incompatible with proper labour discipline and with the "march of progress".'[21]

The introduction of machinery resulted in employers needing greater control over working hours. While this transformation was less rapid in rural areas it had certainly occurred by the middle of the century. Three basic methods of time discipline were used by employers: deterrents, wage incentives, and the formulation of a new work ethos. Deterrents were most common during the early years of the century, with wage incentives being used more frequently by the mid 19th century. The creation of a new work ethos was more subtle and included the use of elementary schools and Sunday schools to inculcate notions of time discipline. This triumph of 'Victorian values' involved the destruction of old popular culture and its replacement by organized recreation, including the growth of spectator sports such as cricket and football, and subsidised outings by train. Seemingly unrelated changes at the national level had a significant impact on aspects of popular culture and local social life. The improvement in transport and communications and the availability of a national press led to the farmer, in particular, being influenced far more by national considerations than had previously been the case. By the 1860s, Stovin at Binbrook Hall could keep 'up to date with social and political events by reading "The Standard" and "The Daily News", which were delivered from the Binbrook Post Office by mail cart, and a fairly wide range of periodicals, some of which were delivered by post and some of which he regularly looked at in the Louth Mechanics Institute Reading Room'. Such influences led to a progressive erosion of locally-held common values and resulted in increased social distancing between the classes within society.[22]

However, it would be wrong to characterize all social relations as being increasingly distanced. The wealthier farmers were expected to provide charity in a similar way to the clergy and gentry. This often took the form of food, particularly at Christmas and for occasional treats. The *Louth and North Lincolnshire Advertiser* summed up popular expectations in 1861 when it reported:

> one of our wold farmers has given his wealthy neighbours an example of benevolence which is not only highly honourable in itself, but worthy of the imitation of all who are placed in similar circumstances. A beast weighing 56 stones has been slaughtered by Mr J. R. King of North Ormsby and distributed among his labourers and poor neighbours who will doubtless appreciate such a charitable act at this festive season of the year.[23]

At Kelstern, Coates Sharpley 'gave all his workers good English beef'. Generosity of this kind was by no means exceptional. Farmers would hold harvest suppers for their labourers. At South Elkington, the Smyths continued this tradition throughout the century, although more generally the practice appears to have been dying out. Labourers might be given a day trip to the coast; Stovin for instance: 'gave his labourers a holiday, sending them and their wives and families to Cleethorpes free of all cost, substantial refreshments were sent with them'. A similar treat was laid on by the Fieldsends at Kirmond Le Mire. Stovin also gave his men a pig at Christmas.[24]

Some areas of social life appeared, at least superficially, unchanged. Throughout the period, it was the landowning classes and their tenantry that exercised political, economic, and judicial leadership, but in itself the subtle influences that modified their behaviour patterns during the century were bound to have an effect on their attitudes towards aspects of social life. The replacement of the traditional harvest home with the harvest festival, for instance, can be seen as a consequence of the changing values of the farmers and the clergy, thereby imposing a new social form on their workforce, whether this was beneficial to the workers or not.[25]

It is against such a backdrop of steady national transformation that we need to consider social life in the villages of the Lincolnshire Wolds. Once again, it quickly becomes apparent that the size of a village had a significant influence on the nature of its social life.

The greater social and economic diversity in the larger villages led to a much wider range of interests and reduced the likelihood of dominance, economic, social or otherwise, by one particular group. At the same time, larger villages had better communications and contacts with the outside world. This in turn led to a more varied culture with greater access to external influences when compared to the more isolated, and therefore more insular, smaller villages.

Where one person owned all the property in a parish he could exercise dictatorial powers should he choose to do so, and such communities were often firmly regulated by the squire and his agent. The Yarboroughs, for instance, required occupiers of field gardens on the estate to cultivate the land by spade husbandry (to encourage manual labour) and prevented them from working the land on Sundays. Cottages in Brocklesby village were carefully designed with main doors at the side, rather than the front, so that visitors passing through the estate would not witness gossiping on doorsteps. In the case of Brocklesby, Yarborough effectively ignored all the poor law legislation, as his agent explained: 'The Earl of Yarborough is the sole owner of all the property within the parish and maintains the poor at his own expense – No poor Rate is ever made and there has not been any recent valuation under the provisions of the Parochial Assessment Act or otherwise.'[26]

The occupants of such parishes were undoubtedly more privileged materially, enjoying a significantly higher quality of life than their counterparts elsewhere. Labourers in these villages were also considered of a higher class:

> The wives of such labourers as occupy cottages in Wold parishes in this district ... [Wold Newton, a parish owned by Lord Yarborough] ... are a grade higher than the class from which public

gangs are recruited, and to get them to work regularly in a private gang could only be accomplished by an amount of coercion.[27]

The larger villages contained a greater proportion of tradesmen than the close parishes, while its agricultural labour force was dominated by the poorer-paid day-labourers rather than the better-off confined men. The two groups co-existed, but in many ways their activities were diametrically opposed.

The casual labourer was largely responsible for the less 'acceptable' aspects of the culture of the larger villages. Much of this can be related to the nature of the labour force and their living conditions, with the concentration of the worst paid and underemployed in the larger villages. The more traditional aspects of popular culture appear to have lingered longer in the larger villages than elsewhere. In Nettleton, the village feast before 1837 was 'for the amusement of holiday folk craving and celebrated for their gastric and bacchanalian pleasures. The further desecration of the sabbath has been by the erection of stalls, for the sinister purpose of selling profitable articles.'[28]

Behaviour in these villages appears to have been generally less respectable, at least in the eyes of the middle-class, town-based, local press. In many ways, the larger villages were similar to the smaller market towns such as Market Rasen, Caistor, and Horncastle where, contrary to myths of Victorian respectability, drunkenness, prostitution, and rowdiness were part and parcel of everyday life. At Tealby, for instance, there were complaints about the conduct of the beer shops and the behaviour of gangs of youths marauding the streets on the Sabbath hurling insults at passers-by. Binbrook was a principal centre for gangs of gypsies. In 1844, 'A sort of stationary rendezvous is kept up at Binbrook, where they herd by scores at different periods of the year, whilst every lane bears the marks of their camps and fires, not withstanding boards containing threats of prosecution may be seen close to the places where they pitch their tents.'[29]

In 1846, some villagers objected to the joining of the two parishes of St Mary and St Gabriel, considering more religious activity was needed 'to check the prevailing and growing vices of the villagers, drunkenness, sabbath breaking, rioting etc were … stated to be rampant

Particularly in the small villages, the church was the central point of the parish. The squire and the parson were principal residents and the villagers dutifully attended church each Sunday. In these villages, the church further reinforced and legitimized the social hierarchy. For the larger villages, it was often the chapel which served spiritual and social needs, while a surprising number attended both. Indeed, on the day of the religious census of 1851, 48 percent of the entire population of the Wolds attended either church or chapel.[57]

In Lincolnshire in 1851, the Church of England had 51 percent of all sittings, less than the national average, but still an indicator of its strength as a single body when compared to the more fragmented nature of other branches of Christianity. On the Lincolnshire Wolds though, Methodism was stronger than Anglicanism. 9,273 (44.6%) people attended Anglican services whilst 11,498 (55.4%) attended Methodist services. However, there were variations across the Wolds. In the towns, the Methodists heavily outnumbered the Anglicans. In Horncastle, nonconformists attending chapel exceeded Anglicans by 50 percent. Over the northern part of the Wolds, the Methodists were in the ascendancy (see Table 6.2) with the Wesleyans outnumbering the

Table 6.2   Religious attendance on the Lincolnshire Wolds, 1851

Area	*C. of E.*	*Primitve*	*Wesleyan*	*Independent*	*Methodist %*
North	1,615	884	1,863	231	65
North-central	1,113	477	974	140	59
Central	1,118	520	996	-	58
South-central	1,835	137	1,001	-	37
South	3,592	444	3,426	405	54
Overall	9,273	2,462	8,260	776	55

Source: Figures taken from R. W. Ambler (ed.), *Lincolnshire returns of the Census of Religious Worship, 1851,* Fakenham, 1979

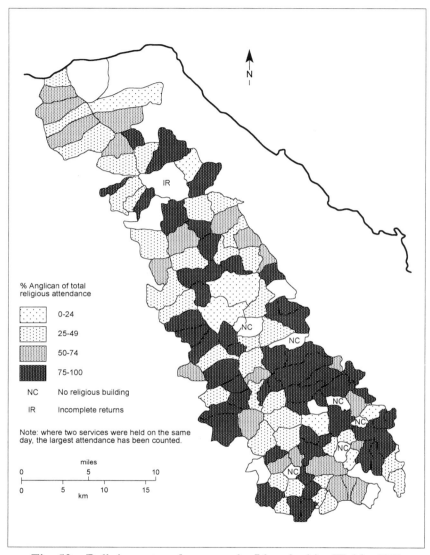

Fig. 50   Religious attendance on the Lincolnshire Wolds, 1851
Source: Drawn from data in R. W. Ambler (ed.),
Lincolnshire returns of the Census of Religious Worship 1851

Primitives by almost two to one. In the villages of the southern Wolds,
Methodists were less strong and the Primitives were outnumbered by

the Wesleyans in the order of eight to one. As can be seen from Figure 50, whole areas of the southern Wolds had little or no nonconformist provision, while in a small number of larger villages in the centre and north, such as Ludford, Binbrook, and Keelby, the Anglicans were very much in the minority.[58]

The 1851 Census provides a snapshot on one particular day, and so its figures should be treated with circumspection. The rector of Swaby, for instance, explained his lowered attendance by reference to the lambing season, 'when the sheep require attendance day and night, and excessive fatigue of harvest to men, women and children'. Nevertheless, the figures do provide a useful overview of religious attendance in mid-century.[59]

The 19th century saw the rise of Methodism as a major force in Christian worship and as a principal contributor to the national way of life, encouraging new approaches to living and, in many cases, providing an influential vehicle for people who previously had little impact on societal development. It was not a coincidence, for instance, that many of the leaders of the first agricultural trade unions came from Methodist backgrounds, as it was the chapel which first gave them their voice and an opportunity to organize aspects of their lives in ways which had not been possible previously. It is beyond the scope of this book to look at the reasons for the rise of Methodism in the 19th century. However, it is fair to say that parts of Lincolnshire proved to be very receptive to the new chapels that were set up as an alternative to the established church.[60]

A brief look at a couple of examples of the growth of Methodism in Lincolnshire villages well illustrates a phenomenon which was found throughout the Wolds. In the large village of Binbrook, Methodists worshipped as early as 1775, by 1800 there were 34 members, a figure which grew rapidly to 93 by 1812. The first Wesleyan chapel was opened in 1816 on the High Street. In addition there were several houses and barns that were registered as places of religious worship during the 1820s and 1830s. Membership continued to grow, reaching 200 in 1849. By 1851, Wesleyan congregations were significantly larger than those in the parish church and Methodism had become the dominant religion in the village. The split that resulted from the Reform

Movement led to the establishment of the Free Methodists in the village in the 1850s. However, despite this setback, Methodist numbers continued to grow and a new chapel was opened in 1878.[61]

The Primitive Methodists built their first chapel in Binbrook in 1836 when their membership was 20. By 1849, numbers had grown to 44, and figures between 40 and 50 are then recorded for the rest of the century. In 1879, a second Primitive chapel was built in a prime position in the Market Place.

The Free Methodists broke away from the Wesleyans at the beginning of the 1850s. A meeting was held in Binbrook in 1853 at which 300 supporters were present. A new chapel with 500 sittings was built in 1855. Membership in 1867 was 135. In 1884, the Free Methodists took delivery of a new harmonium manufactured by Mr J. Reed of London which was 'said to be the largest delivered at Louth Station'. However, by 1891 the numbers of Free Methodists had declined to 99. [62]

The development of the chapels in Binbrook was by no means exceptional. In the space of 62 years, five chapels were built, with each successive one being larger and grander than the previous building. Membership of the various chapels was generally around 250 in a village whose peak population was only 1,334 in 1861. This is a striking figure, since it has been estimated that there were usually about four times as many adherents as members. This figure suggests that the village was also acting as a central village for the provision of Methodist worship not available in some of the smaller surrounding villages such as Kirmond Le Mire and Swinhope.[63]

A second example serves to reinforce the impression of the growth of nonconformity. In Keelby, Methodism was also in the ascendant. At the time of the 1851 religious census, about 85 percent of religious attendance was at nonconformist chapels. In common with Binbrook, the Methodists embarked on a series of building programmes during the century. The original Methodist chapel was built in 1824 and enlarged in 1829. A second Wesleyan chapel was opened in 1844 and a third and larger chapel capable of holding 400 was built in 1867. The Primitive Methodists started in a labourer's house in 1828 and built their first chapel in 1836, replacing it in 1850 with a larger chapel.[64]

year at Thornton Abbey; Russell, *Water drinkers,* pp.18–19, 74, 77.
Lord Worsley (son of Yarborough) gave £5 to the Temperance
Library in Louth. Sir Culling Eardley Smith addressed a meeting of
teetotallers in Nettleton. Russell, *Water drinkers*, pp. 10–11.

36   *LRSM*, 14 February 1851.
37   ibid., 14 February 1851. Nettleton WEA, *Aspects*, pp. 23–4.
38   *LRSM*, 12 June 1840.
39   Gosden, *Friendly societies,* pp. 33, 43.
40   *LRSM*, 14 July 1865 quoted in R. C. Russell, *Friendly societies in the Caistor, Binbrook and Brigg area in the nineteenth century*, Nettleton, 1975, p. 9.
41   *LRSM*, 20 July 1860.
42   ibid., 20 July 1883. For a more detailed discussion of the Foresters in Keelby see Rawding, *Keelby*, ch. 11.
43   Tealby School Log Book, cited in Russell, *Friendly societies*, p. 4. Tealby School Log Book, 18 June 1888, 20 June 1897.
44   Rawding, *Keelby,* particularly ch. 9. Russell, *Water drinkers,* p. 11.
45   *LRSM*, 21 July 1871 cited in Russell, *Friendly societies,* p. 3.
46   *GFP*, 6 July 1860.
47   *MRWM*, 17 December 1859, *LNLA*, 2 November 1861, 8 November 1862.
48   Russell, *Revolt of the Field*, p. 166, N. A. D. Scotland, 'The role of Methodism in the origin and development of the revolt of the field in Lincolnshire, Norfolk and Suffolk 1872–1896', PhD thesis, University of Aberdeen, 1975 p. 454.
49   *LNLA*, 4 March 1860.
50   J. Bishop: 'Barton on Humber Literary Institute', *Lincs P & P*, 26 (1996–7), pp. 8–12.
51   *MRWM,* 4 March 1865, 25 March 1865, 15 January 1861, 31 January 1863.
52   Russell, *Friendly societies*, pp. 52–6.
53   Russell, *Revolt of the Field.*
54   D. N. Robinson, *The book of Louth*, Buckingham, 1979, pp. 111, 120, D. G. Boyce, *An early Victorian Market Town: Market Rasen in the 1850s*, Market Rasen, 1996, p. 112, J. Lucas, *Market Rasen Races*, Buckingham, 1989, pp. 22–8, Russell, *Revolt of the Field*, pp. 52–6. *LNLA*, 5 April 1884, 7 April 1888.
55   *LNLA*, 9 August 1884.
56   F. Knight, *The nineteenth century church and English society*, Cambridge, 1993, pp. 70–1.

57   Out of a total population of 43,655, 20,771 were counted as attending
      either church or chapel. Such figures should be treated with
      circumspection; however, they do give a clear indication of the high
      level of religious attendance by modern standards, even if at the time
      they were seen rather more as a sign of religious and moral decline by
      contemporary commentators, For an overview see O. Chadwick, *The
      Victorian Church*, Parts I & II, London, 1966, 1970.
58   *Lincolnshire returns of the Census of Religious Worship, 1851*, ed. R. W.
      Ambler, Fakenham, 1979.
59   Ambler, *Census*, p. 61.
60   On Methodism see Ambler, *Ranters*, and Obelkevich, *Religion*, chs. 4
      and 5.
61   DISS 1/177/5/3; PRO. HO 129/431, cited in *Labouring life on the
      Lincolnshire Wolds: a study of Binbrook in the mid nineteenth century*, ed. R. J.
      Olney, Nottingham, 1975. LAO. FB5 364. Watchman, 1878, p. 216.
62   *LRSM*, 18 March 1853. *L.C.*, 17 August 1855. *Binbrook in the nineteenth
      century*, ed. C. Rawding, Binbrook, 1989, ch. 7.
63   Rawding, *Binbrook*.
64   Rawding, *Keelby*.
65   ibid., p. 63.
66   Scotland, 'The role of Methodism', p. 85. Obelkevich, *Religion*, p. 245.
67   N. A. D. Scotland, 'Methodism and the revolt of the field in East
      Anglia, 1872–96', *Proceedings of the Wesley Historical Society*, 41 (1977), p. 9.
68   Obelkevich, *Religion*, p. 168.
69   Tealby School Log Book, 20 July 1899.
70   LAO. COR B5/4/64/4/37, 22 January 1842. Letter from Johnson
      Grant to Robert Johnson, 28 July 1842. CP. For a more detailed
      discussion of the conflict between the Binbrook clergy and vestry see
      C. K. Rawding, 'To the glory of God?' *LHA*, 25 (1990), pp. 41–6.

CONCLUSION

For much of the 19th century, the Lincolnshire Wolds was a region which was quite distinct in many ways from the rest of rural England. At the beginning of the century, it was an agricultural backwater, characterized by low productivity sheep walks on thin chalky soils, small villages nestling in valleys where water was available, and large landed estates that had yet to develop their agricultural potential.

By the middle years of the century, the area had been transformed, catapulted into the vanguard of agricultural innovation with its highly regarded mixed farming system. The key to this transformation's taking place lay in the relationship between landowners and tenant farmers, and most specifically in the nature of the tenantry at that time. The changes were possible due to the timely coincidence of a range of factors: high grain prices along with low rental levels, agricultural innovations which made lighter soils a more viable proposition, and a landownership structure and farm-size pattern which was well suited to the effective introduction of the new technologies. As such, conditions were much more suitable for the development of advanced capitalist farms worked by a waged agricultural labour force than was the case in areas such as the Lincolnshire marsh and fens.

In many ways during the middle years of the century, the Lincolnshire Wolds epitomized the 'Golden Age' of British farming, as the technology-based dreams of writiers such as Arthur Young appeared to be realized through a judicious mixture of enlightened landownership policies, joint investment by landlord and tenant, and favourable economic conditions.

The pattern of population distribution also aided developments. A few larger villages, relatively evenly spaced, enabled a labour market to develop which was extremely favourable to the farmer in the smaller, more isolated settlements on the tops of the Wolds. He was able to operate with a permanent well-paid core workforce resident in close proximity to the farm while calling on a pool of day labourers and casual workers who were obliged to walk from their homes in the nearest larger villages.

At the same time, these larger villages were able to develop as specialist service centres supporting the farming of the surrounding parishes. The absence of any significant elements of manufacturing industry and the limited improvements to transport technology on the Wolds meant that a system developed which was all but purely agricultural in focus.

By the middle years of the century, the distinctiveness of the region was beginning to fade. By now, the Wolds could be categorized with the arable growing counties of eastern England, all of which shared similar farming practices. The distribution of labour which had so favoured the farmers was now presenting problems of labour supply as the economy became more nationally based and workers gained greater awareness of economic opportunities both in the towns and further afield.

Nevertheless, agriculture continued to develop steadily until the depression of the final quarter of the century, when the region was engulfed in the hostile national economic climate which shook farming to its very core and severely undermined all the assumptions on which the previous seventy years of progress had been based. By this time, the picture on the Wolds was very similar to that of much of eastern England: farmers under pressure, landlords selling up, labourers leaving the land, and the small towns and large villages struggling to sustain their earlier prosperity in the face of economic decline.

The development of a fully integrated national economy and rapidly improving transport and communications links diluted further the distinctiveness of the Wolds. Its society, just like in the rest of rural England, became increasingly responsive to national trends, being incorporated into a wider world drawn together by markets, improved communications, the drift from the countryside to the towns, and the rise of nationally based leisure and recreation.

By 1900, the Lincolnshire Wolds had become a very different place from that of a century before. Yet, by tracing the groups of people through the century and assessing the processes that influenced societal development, it is possible to identify a certain coherence and continuity which gave the area its distinctiveness. The concentration of different groups of people in different villages or on the farms, the varied interest and activities of social groups, and the complex set of interactions between these groups define the 'pays' which was the Lincolnshire Wolds in the 19th century.

BIBLIOGRAPHY

Afton, B, 'The great agricultural depression on the English chalklands: the Hampshire experience', *Agricultural History Review*, 44 (1996), pp. 191–205

Acton, R., 'The Market Rasen Canal, 1801–1908', *Lincolnshire History and Archaeology*, 17 (1982), pp. 61–2

Ambler, R. W. (ed.), *Lincolnshire returns of the Census of Religious Worship*, 1851, Fakenham, 1979

Ambler, R. W., *Ranters, revivalists and reformers,* Hull, 1989

J. Arch, *From ploughtail to parliament. An autobiography*, London, 1986

Archer, J. E., 'Rural protest in Norfolk and Suffolk, 1830–1870', in *Rural social change and conflicts since 1500*, ed. A. Charlesworth, Hull, 1982, pp. 83–95

Armstrong, A., *Farmworkers: a social and economic history, 1770–1980*, London, 1998

Arnold, R., *The farthest promised land*, Wellington, 1981

Barber, S., 'Irish migrant agricultural labourers in nineteenth century Lincolnshire', *Saothar*, 8 (1982), pp. 10–22

Barnes, P., *Norfolk landowers since 1880*, Norwich, 1993

Barnwell, P. S., 'An extra dimension? Lincolnshire farm buildings as historical evidence', *Agricultural History Review*, 46 (1998), pp. 35–46

Barnwell, P. S. and C. Giles, *English farmsteads 1750–1914*, Swindon, 1994

Beastall, T. W., *The agricultural revolution in Lincolnshire*, Lincoln, 1978

Beckett, J. V., 'English rural society 1750–1914', *The Historian*, 38 (1993), pp. 10–12

Beckett, J. V., 'The decline of the small landowner in England and Wales', in *Landowners, capitalists and entrepreneurs*, ed. F. M. L. Thompson, Oxford, 1994

Bennett, E., *Brackenborough: the story of a manor*, Louth, 1995

Bovill, E. W., *The England of Nimrod and Surtees, 1815–1854*, Oxford, 1959

Boyce, G., *An early Victorian market town: Market Rasen in the eighteen fifties*, Market Rasen, 1996

Brown, J. H., 'Agriculture in Lincolnshire during the Great Depression, 1873–1896', PhD thesis, University of Manchester, 1978

Burke, J. B., *A visitation of the seats and arms of the noblemen and gentlemen of Great Britain and Ireland,* London, 1855

Burton, J., *Henry Winn's village*, Fulletby, n.d.

Caird, J., *English agriculture in 1850–51*, London, 1968

Cameron, D. K., *The English fair*, Stroud, 1998

Chadwick, O., *The Victorian church*, Parts I & II, London, 1966, 1970

Clarke, J. A., *On the farming of Lincolnshire. Prize essay*, London, 1852

Clarke, J. N., 'Horncastle Baptists', *Lincolnshire Past and Present*, 40 (2000), pp. 6–9

Clemenson, H. A., *English country houses and landed estates*, London, 1982

Clifford, S., *Local distinctiveness: place, particularity, and identity*, London, 1993

Collins, E. J. T., 'Migrant labour in British agriculture in the nineteenth century', *Economic History Review*, 29 (1976), pp. 38–59

Collins, G. E., *Farming and fox hunting*, n.d.

Collins, G. E., *History of the Brocklesby hounds, 1700–1901*, London, 1902

Countryside Commission, *The Lincolnshire Wolds landscape*, Banbury, 1993

Darby, H. C., 'The Lincolnshire Wolds', *Lincolnshire Historian*, 9 (1952), pp. 315–24

Darley, G., *Villages of vision*, London, 1975

Davey, B., *Lawless and immoral: policing a country town 1838–1857*, Leicester, 1983

Dentith, S., *Social and cultural forms in nineteenth century England,* London, 1998

Doris, R. F., 'Portraits in stone', *Lincolnshire Life,* April 1978, pp. 27–9

Dunbabin, J. P. D., *Rural discontent in nineteenth century Britain,* London, 1974

Fisher, J. R., 'Landowners and English tenant right, 1854–1852', *Agricultural History Review,* 31 (1983), pp. 15–25

Frankish, W., 'Report of the Steward of Implements', *Journal of the Royal Agricultural Society of England,* 2nd ser., 16 (1880), pp. 177–94

Frost, K. A., 'When trains ran to Spilsby', *Lincolnshire Life,* July 1968

Fuller, H. A., 'Landownership and the Lindsey landscape', *Annals of the Association of American Georgraphers,* 66 (1976), pp. 14–23

Girouard, M. *The Victorian country house,* Yale, 1971

Girouard, M., *Return to Camelot,* Yale, 1981

Gregory, D., 'The friction of distance? Information circulation and the mails in early nineteenth century England', *Journal of Historical Geography,* 13 (1987), pp. 130–45

Grigg, D. B., 'The development of tenant right in south Lincolnshire', *Lincolnshire Historian,* 2 (1962), pp. 41–8

Grigg, D. B., 'An index of regional change in English farming', *Transactions of the Institute of British Geographers,* 36 (1965), pp. 55–67

Grigg, D. B., 'Farm size in England and Wales, from early Victorian times to the present', *Agricultural History Review,* 35 (1987), pp. 179–89

Golby, J. M. (ed.), *Culture and society in Britain, 1850–1900,* Oxford, 1986

Gosden, P. H. J. H., *The friendly societies in England 1815–1875,* Manchester, 1961

Haggard, H. Rider, *A farmer's year,* London, 1987

Hall, A., 'Fenland worker-peasants. The economy of smallholders at Rippingale, Lincolnshire, 1791–1871', *Agricultural History Review,* Suppl. ser., 1 (1992)

Hall, S., 'Notes on deconstructing the popular', in *People's history and socialist theory,* ed. R. Samuel, London, 1981

Harding, N. S. (ed.), *Bonney's Church notes*, Lincoln, 1935

Hasbach, W., *A history of the English agricultural labourer*, London, 1920

Hempton, D., *Methodism and politics in British society, 1750–1850*, London, 1987

Higgs, E., 'Occupational censuses and the agricultural workforce in Victorian England and Wales', *Economic History Review*, 48 (1995), pp. 700–16

Hobsbawm, E. (ed.), *The invention of tradition*, Cambridge, 1983

Hobsbawm, E. and G. Rudé, *Captain Swing*, Harmondsworth, 1985

Hocken, J., *A brief history of Wesleyan Methodism in the Grimsby Circuit*, Grimsby, 1839

Holderness, B. A., 'Open and close parishes in England in the eighteenth and nineteenth centuries', *Agricultural History Review*, 20 (1972), pp. 126–39

Holderness, B. A., 'Rural society in SE Lindsey, 1660–1840', PhD thesis, University of Nottingham, 1968

Horn, P., *The changing countryside in Victorian and Edwardian England and Wales*, London, 1984

Howkins, A., 'The discovery of rural England', in *Englishness: politics and culture 1880–1920*, eds. R. Colls and P. Dodd, London, 1987

Howkins, A., *Reshaping rural England*, London, 1991

Howkins, A., 'Peasants, servants and labourers: the marginal workforce in British agriculture c. 1970–1914', *Agricultural History Review*, 42 (1994), pp. 49–62

Imray, J. 'The Boucheretts', *Lincolnshire Historian*, 2 (1955–56), pp. 11–23

Jefferies, R., *Hodge and his masters*, London, 1966

Jenkins, H. M., 'Aylesby, Riby and Rothwell farms near Grimsby, Lincolnshire in the occupation of Mr William Torr', *Journal of the Royal Agricultural Society of England*, 2nd ser., 5 (1869), pp. 415–42

Johnson, J. H., 'Harvest migration from nineteenth century Ireland', *Transactions of the Institute of British Geographers*, 41 (1967), pp. 97–112

Knight, F., *The nineteenth century Church and English society*, Cambridge, 1995

Kightly, C., *Country voices*, London, 1984

Kussmaul, A., *Servants in husbandry in early modern England*, Cambridge, 1981

Leach, T. R., *Lincolnshire country houses and their families, part two*, Dunholme, 1991

Leach, T. R. and R. Pacey, *Lost Lincolnshire country houses*, vol. 2, Burgh Le Marsh, 1992

Leary, W., *Lincolnshire Methodism*, Buckingham, 1988

Lester, G., *Grimsby Methodism and the Wesleys in Lincolnshire*, London, 1890

Levy, D. H., *Large and small holdings*, Cambridge, 1911

Linstrum, D., *Sir Jeffry Wyatville, architect to the king*, Oxford, 1972

Londonderry, the Marchioness of, *Henry Chaplin, a memoir*, London, 1926

Lowerson, J., 'The aftermath of Swing: anti-poor law movements and rural trades unions in the south-east of England', in *Rural social change and conflicts since 1500*, ed. A. Charlesworth, Hull, 1982

Malcolmson, R. W., *Popular recreations in English society, 1700–1850*, Cambridge, 1973

Martineau, H., 'A cameo of Caistor', *Lincolnshire Life*, January 1972

Mills, D. R., *Lord and peasant in nineteenth century Britain*, London, 1980

Mills, D. R., 'Country seats of the gentry', in *An historical atlas of Lincolnshire*, eds. S. Bennett and N. Bennett, Hull, 1993

Mills, D. R. and K. Schurer (eds.), *Local communities in the Victorian Census Enumerators Books*, Oxford, 1996

Mingay, G. E., *Rural life in Victorian England*, Stroud, 1990

Mitson, A. and B. Cox, 'Victorian estate housing on the Yarborough estate, Lincolnshire', *Rural History*, 6 (1995), pp. 29–45

Monson, John Ninth Lord (ed.), *Lincolnshire church notes made by William John Monson, 1828–1840*, Hereford, 1936

Moses, G., '"Rustic and rude": hiring fairs and their critics in East Yorkshire c. 1850–75', *Rural History*, 7 (1996), pp. 151–75

Nettleton WEA, *Aspects of life and work in Nettleton in the nineteenth century*, Nettleton, 1980

Obelkevich, J., *Religion and rural society, South Lindsey 1825–1875*, Oxford, 1976

Irwin, C. S., 'The history of tenant right', *The Estate Magazine*, 39 (1939), pp. 198–202

Olney, R. J., *Lincolnshire politics*, Oxford, 1973

Olney, R. J. (ed.), *Labouring life on the Lincolnshire Wolds: a study of Binbrook in the mid nineteenth century*, Nottingham, 1975

Olney, R. J., *Rural society and county government in nineteenth century Lincolnshire*, Lincoln, 1979

Overton, M., 'Agriculture', in *Atlas of industrialising Britain, 1780–1914*, eds. J. Langton and R. J. Morris, London, 1986

Overton, M., *Agricultural Revolution in England: the transformation of the agrarian economy, 1500–1850*, Cambridge, 1996

Pashley, R., *Pauperism and poor laws*, London, 1852

Perkins, J. A., 'Harvest technology and labour supply in Lincolnshire and the East Riding of Yorkshire, 1750–1850', *Labour and Tillage*, 3 (1976), pp. 47–58, 125–35

Perkins, J. A., 'The prosperity of farming on the Lindsey uplands, 1813–1837', *Agricultural History Review*, 24 (1976), pp. 126–43

Perkins, J. A., 'Unmarried mothers and the poor law in Lincolnshire, 1800–1850', *Lincolnshire History and Archaeology*, 20 (1985), pp. 21–33

Perron, R., *Agriculture in depression, 1870–1940,* Cambridge, 1995

Pevsner, N. and J. Harris, *The buildings of Lincolnshire*, London, 1989

Phythian-Adams, C., *Rethinking English local history*, Leicester, 1987

Porter, J. H., 'The revolt of the field: the Devon response', *Southern History*, 7 (1985), pp. 163–78

Pusey, P., 'On the agricultural improvements of Lincolnshire', *Journal of the Royal Agricultural Society of England*, 4 (1843), pp. 287–316

Rawding, C. K., 'Poor relief and the rural workforce: a case study of north Lincolnshire, 1834–1861', University of Sussex research paper in Geography, 16 (1986)

Rawding, C. K. (ed.), *Keelby parish and people. Part two 1831–1881*, Keelby, 1987

Rawding, C. K., 'The poor law amendment act 1834–65: a case study of Caistor poor law union', *Lincolnshire History and Archaeology*, 22 (1987), pp. 15–23

Rawding, C. K. (ed.), *Binbrook in the nineteenth century*, Binbrook, 1989

Rawding, C. K., 'The iconography of churches: a case study of landownership and power in nineteenth century north Lincolnshire', *Journal of Historical Geography*, 16 (1990), pp. 157–76

Rawding, C. K., 'To the glory of God?', *Lincolnshire History and Archaeology*, 25 (1990), pp. 41–5

Rawding, C. K., *Binbrook 1900–1939*, Binbrook, 1991

Rawding, C. K., 'Society and place in nineteenth century north Lincolnshire', *Rural History*, 3 (1992), pp. 59–67

Rawding, C. K., 'Agricultural land use in 1801', in *An historical atlas of Lincolnshire,* eds. S. Bennett and N. Bennett, Hull, 1993, pp. 92–3

Rawding, C. K., 'Village type and employment structure: an analysis in the nineteenth century Lincolnshire Wolds', *Local Population Studies*, 53 (1994), pp. 53–69

Rawding, C. K. and B. Short, 'Binbrook in 1910: the use of the Finance (1909–1910) Act Records', *Lincolnshire History and Archaeology*, 28 (1993), pp. 58–65

Redford, A., *Labour migration in England 1800–1850*, Manchester, 1976

Reed, M. 'The peasantry of nineteenth century England, a neglected class?', *History Workshop*, 18 (1984), pp. 53–74

Reed, M., 'Indoor farm service in nineteenth century Sussex: some criticisms of a critique', *Sussex Archaeological Collections*, 123 (1985), pp. 225–41

Reed, M. and R. Wells, 'An agenda for modern rural history?', in *Class conflict and protest in the English countryside 1700–1880,* eds. M. Reed and R. Wells, London, 1990

INDEX

Goulceby, 53, 78
Grant, Johnson, 222
Great Grimsby and Sheffield
  Junction Railway Company, 41
Great Limber, 56, 71, 75, 81, 82,
  96, 117, 119, 121, 157, 213
Great Northern Railway, 42–3
Great Sturton, 30
Grimsby, 36, 143
Gulson, Edward, 135

H
Haggard, Rider, 156, 190
Hagworthingham, 53
Hainton, 51, 65–6, 74, 84, 140
Hallington, 131–2
Hameringham, 78
Handson, Henry, 106–7
Harneis family, 70, 76, 172
Harrington, 56, 79, 177
Harvest homes, 220–1
Hatcliffe, 3, 84, 154
Haugham, 67, 79
Hawerby, 141, 172
Heneage family, 41, 51–2, 65–6, 74,
  81, 84, 102, 117, 138, 158, 187,
  189
Holdgate, of Thoresway, 16
Holiwell, George, 70
Holt, J. M., the Revd, 210
Horkstow, 175, 188
Horncastle, 23, 37, 38, 40, 53, 147,
  150, 201, 202, 208
Horncastle Horse Association, 148
Horncastle Horse Fair, 203–4
Horncastle Navigation, 41
River Humber, 39
Huntley, J. T., 161

I
Iles family, 103, 108, 120, 129, 134
Incorporated Church Building
  Society, 79
Irby, 78, 97

K
Kaye, Bishop John, 70, 79, 216,
  222
Keelby, 81, 104, 149, 154, 158–9,
  181–4, 212, 213, 219, 220–1
Kelstern, 14, 19, 114, 129, 131,
  173, 206
Killingholme, 110
Kirmington, 60, 71
Kirmond Le Mire, 19, 30, 82, 148,
  183, 187, 206, 220
Kirwin, Mr, 130

L
Laceby, 154
Langton by Spilsby, 54, 74
Langton family, 54, 68
Lincoln, 36
Lincoln Assizes, 147
Lincolnshire Chamber of
  Agriculture, 134
Lincolnshire General servants
  Amelioration Society, 142
Lincolnshire Labour Emigration
  and Migration League, 154
Little Cawthorpe, 19
Little Carlton, 142
Livesey family, 30
Louth, 36–7, 39, 40, 43–6, 84, 130,
  141, 143, 147, 160, 182, 186, 200,
  212, 214, 215, 216
Louth Poor Law Union, 87–8, 186,